PRAISE FOR

how to be a sister

"A MARVELOUS, HARROWING, life-affirming book. In looking to forge a meaningful relationship with her severely autistic sister, Eileen Garvin finds a simpler way of being in, and extending, every moment. Isn't that what we're all after? I loved this book. And boy, can she write!"

—ABIGAIL THOMAS, AUTHOR OF
A Three Dog Life: A Memoir

"AUTISTIC KIDS GROW up to be autistic adults. They have brothers and sisters who grow up alongside them. This book is an unforgettable, courageous, and explicit sibling's eye view into a rarely explored relationship, where the bond wrought by love and joy, crisis and heartbreak is mesmerizing."

—MARY-ANN TIRONE SMITH, AUTHOR OF
Girls of Tender Age: A Memoir

"ALTHOUGH EILEEN GARVIN was the younger sister, she was expected to be responsible for Margaret. Now, as an adult, Eileen struggles to understand her unpredictable and effusive sister, and finds that no matter how much confusion and inner conflict she feels, she always returns to love. A poignant, thoughtful, and honest portrayal of life with a sibling who has autism."

—RACHEL SIMON, AUTHOR OF *Riding the Bus with My Sister*
and *Building a Home with My Husband*

THE EXPERIMENT

BECAUSE EVERY BOOK IS A TEST OF NEW IDEAS

"HOW TO BE A SISTER, told with amazing insight and compassion, is rich in the hilarious detail of coping with a beloved family member with special needs. Read this book. It will enrich your life."

—TERRELL HARRIS DOUGAN, AUTHOR OF
That Went Well: Adventures in Caring for My Sister

"EILEEN GARVIN'S PORTRAITS of her sister Margaret in chaotic action bring a rich identity into focus, an identity that includes autism—but also a wild and playful tug-of-war with the world that more truly defines Margaret. Bravo to Eileen for seeing and for enabling the rest of us to witness her sister's creativity, purpose, and profoundly independent path."

—JUDY KARASIK, COAUTHOR OF *The Ride Together:
A Brother and Sister's Memoir of Autism in the Family*

"EILEEN GARVIN HAS written a deeply reflective, generous book about her relationship with her older sister, Margaret, who has autism. A compelling description of how Garvin's childhood experiences continued to influence her interactions with her sister many years later, it gracefully intertwines humor, pain, respect, and optimism. Eileen Garvin is open about her struggles, her love, her anger, her guilt, her fear, and her respect for her sister—as a child and as a woman. Every parent who is raising both a child with autism and a neurotypical child should read this book. So should every older teen or adult sibling of a person with autism. And so should all the rest of us who want to gain a greater empathy for the life of a family which includes a child with autism."

—SANDRA L. HARRIS, PHD, EXECUTIVE DIRECTOR, DOUGLASS
DEVELOPMENTAL DISABILITIES CENTER, RUTGERS UNIVERSITY, AND
COAUTHOR OF *Siblings of Children with Autism: A Guide for Families*

how to be a sister

eileen garvin

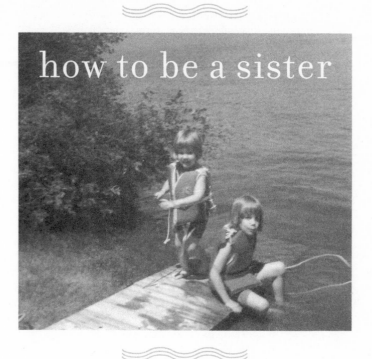

how to be a sister

A LOVE STORY
WITH
A TWIST *of* AUTISM

THE EXPERIMENT
NEW YORK

THE EXPERIMENT, LLC
260 FIFTH AVENUE
NEW YORK, NY 10001-6425
WWW.THEEXPERIMENTPUBLISHING.COM

Grateful acknowledgment is made for permission to reprint a portion of the lyrics to "Mack the Knife" on pages 25–26:

English Words by Marc Blitzstein
Original German Words by Bert Brecht
Music by Kurt Weill
© 1928 (Renewed) Universal Edition
© 1955 (Renewed) Weill-Brecht-Harms Co., Inc.
Renewal Rights Assigned to the Kurt Weill Foundation for Music,
Bert Brecht
and
The Estate of Marc Blitzstein
All Rights Administered by WB Music Corp.
All Rights Reserved

LIBRARY OF CONGRESS Control Number: 2009940033

ISBN 978-1-61519-016-4

COVER DESIGN BY Alison Forner
COVER AND AUTHOR photographs by Stacey Adams
TITLE PAGE PHOTOGRAPH by Lawrence T. Garvin
of Eileen (left) and Margaret, 1974
TEXT DESIGN BY Pauline Neuwirth, Neuwirth & Associates, Inc.

MANUFACTURED IN THE United States of America
FIRST PRINTING APRIL 2010
10 9 8 7 6 5 4 3 2 1

For Brendan

contents

how to be a sister

1.

family-style dining

*Children should be taught to speak quietly, and to use their
best manners so that this experience is as pleasurable for
other restaurant patrons as it is for your family.*

—*On Dining Out*, EMILY POST'S ETIQUETTE

THROUGHOUT THE COURSE of my life, I've only been
certain of two things: I am the youngest of five children, and I am my sister Margaret's older sister. Even
though she was born three years earlier than I, I was the
caretaker, the dependable one, and, as far as I can see,
always will be. Instead of growing up in the protective
shadow of my big sister, I often found myself dodging
things she was throwing at me or chasing that shadow
through a crowd of people as my big sister took off on
some crazy escapade.

Margaret and I did not choose this role reversal. You
could say that her autism assigned it to us. For as long

as I can remember, I was often in charge of Margaret, who could never be left alone, and so it fell to me to be the responsible party during the frequent social calamities caused by her trespasses during our childhood: her mirthful and public nudity that I struggled to cover; her loud and clear laughter during moments of silence that I tried to hush; or, worse yet, the times that her anxiety and fear turned to uncontrollable screaming that I was powerless to quell.

The passage of time didn't seem to help, and I felt that sense of powerlessness return to me in our adult years. I felt its icy grip one particular June morning as I sat behind the wheel of my mother's car out in front of my sister's house in Spokane, Washington. My mother had lent me the car so that I could take Margaret out to lunch. *Lunch. A lunch date. My sister and I are going out to lunch. I'm in town visiting, and we are going to grab some lunch. Catch up.* In the vocabulary of regular people, this sounded so reasonable, so normal. But where I came from, this was unknown territory that could sooner resemble a riot than two women in their thirties enjoying a midday meal together.

I sat in the car, clutching the wheel, trying to gather my thoughts. I simply didn't know what to expect. I'd been in town for several days and was just now getting over to see Margaret. Even though I had come home expressly to meet with her, I had no idea how this get-together would go and if it would make one or both of us miserable, so I hadn't exactly rushed over to see her. I didn't even know if my sister would get in the car with me, to be perfectly frank, because she is a woman who loves her routine, and this was definitely something new—having me show up at her house in our mother's car and asking her to go somewhere with me alone.

DURING THE PAST few years, my visits home had grown brief and violent. *Violent.* Now that's a word you don't like to hear in relation to family togetherness, but it's the only word that begins to tell the truth. When we gathered at our lakeside cabin, my sister would become, at some point in the weekend, out of control. She would scream, bang the table with her fists, and throw things. She might be set off by some minor disruption—a lost CD, a missing trinket, some undetectable change in the environment. Trying to help my sister in her panic has always felt like coming to the aid of a person whose language I don't speak. She simply cannot put into words the terrible crisis she is in, and I have no way to decipher her need, no matter how dire.

After a while I began to suspect that she wasn't freaking out about any lost item. I started to think she was freaking out because she'd left the safe and careful routine of her group home to be with the rest of us. She was seeing all of us, who had been absent for most of the year, quite suddenly in the same place. It was crowded, noisy, and chaotic, and it pissed her off and stressed her out. That was my theory.

Whatever the case, Margaret would get upset, and

then my father would blow his top. And my mother would let him. Then the rest of us would feel responsible and angry and helpless. The world exploded, and no one ever talked about it. Then all that pain and sadness had nowhere to go. I would climb back on the plane to my home in New Mexico with a headache that lasted for days. I would think about my sister and wonder if it would be better not to see her at all. I would think about the rest of my family and wonder how we could survive this decades-old cycle of destruction.

As I SAT outside Margaret's house in my mother's car, I knew what might happen even if I didn't know what to expect. The possibilities ran rampant in my mind. Dining out with my sister had always been an exceptionally dynamic experience. To begin with, when we were children, eating out was a rare occasion. My parents were always trying to save a buck so that they could put us all through Catholic high school and then college, thereby getting us the hell out of the house. Our infrequent dining out was motivated by mental health issues, too— namely, that taking their five children out in public made my parents want to kill themselves just a little less than they wanted to murder the rest of us.

And to make the understatement of the millennium, I'll say that my sister wasn't at her best in restaurants. Noisy, crowded, unfamiliar places stressed her out. Restaurant dining took her out of her rigid, comforting routine and also away from the short menu of foods she found palatable—spaghetti, macaroni and cheese, and spaghetti.

There was also the matter of interminable waiting at restaurants: waiting to be seated, waiting for menus, waiting to order. Then she had to wait for the food to come, wait for everyone else to finish eating, wait for the check. This entire process was supremely different from Margaret's preferred mode of dining, what we call the Six-and-a-Half-Minute Meal. Three hundred and ninety seconds is all the time it takes for Margaret to charge the table, fill and empty her plate, chug her drink, scramble into her coat while she is still swallowing, and stand by the door waiting to be driven home. "THANKS FOR THE SPA-GHETTI, MOM!" she says in her high monotone voice, waving good-bye to the rest of us, who are still sitting at the table with our forks in the air.

Leisurely dining was never a habit for Margaret, and during our childhood the anxiety she felt in a public dining room was more than palpable to the rest of us. It created a force field of nervous energy that electrified everybody as we waited for, well, everything to fall apart.

With Margaret, not only did these events become greatly accelerated, but sometimes the distinct periods were jumbled out of order. My sister might order dessert in the lobby when the hostess came to tell us our table was almost ready. Or, after clamoring over and over again that she wanted spaghetti, PLEASE, she'd refuse to speak to the waiter who finally came to take our order. And she couldn't tolerate the time lapse between the ordering part and the eating part of dining in a restaurant.

It's not that she was particularly ravenous, either, as she fretted, waiting for the food to appear. She just wanted to get on with things. Her autism didn't let her appreciate the white space, the pause, the invisible transitions between action and rest in everyday activity. So if she wasn't Ordering, by God, she should be Eating. And if she was done Eating, it was time to Go Home. As a result, every moment of such an evening—from the second we climbed into our twelve-passenger Chevy van and clicked into our seat belts until we were safely back at the house—was well seasoned with family-wide anxiety. The rest of us might have wanted to enjoy everything— or anything—that happened in between, but for Margaret the best part of the evening was getting back to the house. The rest of it, on Margaret's terms, was simply a period to be suffered through. And so we all suffered together, as families do.

My other siblings and I pondered the ominous, eternal question, "When will she lose it?" We never thought "why" or "if." We knew from experience that the question was "when." So we ate fast. We ate to a silent but thunderous cadence: "Can-we-get-through-this-before-Margaret-throws-a-fork-and-Dad-makes-us-leave?" Margaret often came unglued right in the middle of dinner, and it was usually my mother who would extract her from the table.

(I've often thought this is why my mother never got fat like other moms; she often didn't get to finish her dinner. She certainly never made it to dessert.) Margaret would get booted for throwing food or silverware or for yelling. Then she'd make a grand exit, sometimes laughing and sometimes kicking and screaming. Or maybe singing. Sometimes she'd even manage to be kicking and screaming while singing and laughing all at the same time. It wasn't all bad; if every head in the restaurant was still turned toward the door my sister had just been dragged through, nobody noticed if I was quietly digging into my spumoni ice cream, which I wasn't supposed to eat because I hadn't finished my dinner. And we never had to wait long for the check, either.

I learned what regular dining was like when I worked in restaurants as a teenager: the process of entering a restaurant, being seated, ordering, and eating was accompanied by quiet conversation and laughter. I observed that this series of events could take anywhere from one to two hours, and that people often seemed relaxed during the entire course of things. It was a joyful experience, a series of pleasant events linked together with harmonious transitions involving small talk, sugar, and salt.

As we grew up, Margaret's tolerance for public dining improved, but she remained predictably unpredictable. And while we might enjoy the kind of amnesia that comes with time and distance, momentarily forgetting how things used to be, it never took a full minute for us to remember just how bad things could get—like the evening my parents took us to a little German café when we were all in our twenties. There were hardly any other diners there that night, and I'd like to think that's why the place ended up closing down, not because of what happened while we were there.

We sat at a long table along one wall, enjoying the atmosphere, chatting and catching up like a normal family. The boys and I had been away at college, and Margaret was living in a group home near my parents' house. We talked and laughed, none of us realizing that Margaret was simmering away at a low boil. Normally she'd clue us into her mood with a minor episode before anything terrible happened. She'd get irritable and maybe stomp her feet or throw something before we left the house, just to let us know she was feeling impatient. This time, however, we were not so lucky. We weren't prepared when she erupted, throwing her linen napkin high in the air and emitting a mind-blowing screech, the kind that should have shattered the crystal. It only lasted for a second, but it seemed to stop time altogether.

I'd been telling some story, and the sound of Margaret's scream just knocked the breath out of me. I felt a slick layer of sweat spring to the surface of my entire body—my scalp, my face, my palms, even the soles of my feet. Across the table the stunned faces of my brothers hung suspended above the tablecloth. At that exact moment a nicely dressed, middle-aged woman had the great misfortune to pass our table. She clutched the back of a chair with one hand. The other hand went to her heart. She gave a little cry and her legs started to buckle. The owner of the restaurant hurried over and helped her back to her own table.

Then life started up again. My brothers and parents and I all breathed in and laughed a little hysterically, happy that we all hadn't, in fact, just been run over by a train or vaporized in a nuclear holocaust, although that's what it had felt like for a second or two. It was just business as usual. My mother patted my sister's hand and told her it was okay. Margaret, looking shaky, took a big drink of water and said, "Okay. That's *good* manners, Mom."

Nobody knew what had set her off, just as none of us knew what had calmed her down. All we knew was that we didn't and couldn't know, but we still felt like we *should* know so that we could keep it from happening in the first place. My brother Larry can still duplicate the noise she made that night, and although I beg him not to, he'll do it every now and then. And then we all laugh and cringe, and I feel like I might cry or throw up, then we laugh some more.

WHEN WE WERE growing up in Spokane, having a relationship with Margaret often felt like living the Bill Murray movie *Groundhog Day*, but without the resolution. The same kinds of things happened over and over again, and we never seemed to get anywhere. These were the questions that weighed heavily on me when I thought about spending time with my sister: What will she do? How will it make me feel? How will it make her feel? We were family, because we were born to the same parents. We were closer to each other genetically than to any other people, but what did that mean, exactly? What was she to me, this person who didn't really have much to say, who seemed to barely tolerate my presence one moment and then turned her bright smile on me the next? And what was I to her?

Autism had made it impossible for us to communicate about any of this. We human beings rely on stories to explain and order our lives. The core of each story remains the same, though we add and subtract layers depending on the audience, the weather, the balance of happiness and sadness on a given day. Margaret's stories remained locked away inside her mind and heart. She tried to explain herself, but she often did not have access to the words, which frustrated her as much as it frustrated the people around her. She had tried to learn some things by rote to give us some satisfaction when we asked, but she often said these things at random, as if searching for what we wanted to hear.

What could I do about any or all of this?

These questions had been much easier to grapple with when I lived sixteen hundred miles away in New Mexico. The distance between us meant I didn't have to do anything. I could just ruminate about Margaret, her autism, and everything that came with it—the guilt, the hilarity, the stress, and the plain bewilderment that had never seemed to diminish over the course of more than thirty years. But now I had decided to move closer to home. So what had been a two-leg airplane trip would soon shrink to an alarmingly short five-hour drive. The move would do away with all the easy excuses that I had never realized I relied on so much—excuses like *Oh, it's so far,* or *I don't have the money to fly,* or *I wish I had more time off.* The truth of the matter is that living so far away had provided me a safe haven from the demands of family and that nagging question that had been with me since birth: Just what are you going to do about Margaret, anyway?

As I SAT there staring at Margaret's front porch, I tried to tell myself I wasn't going to figure it all out at once. That was the idea behind the lunch date—starting with something easy. People often say that if you break a problem down into its parts and deal with one part at a time, what seems impossible is actually easy. But then again, people who talk in clichés are apt to bring up those four blind guys who describe an elephant four different ways, depending on which part each has in his hands. That was a worrisome metaphor, as it made me fear I would never understand this family puzzle until it was too late. And as far as I could tell, an elephant was an elephant no matter which part you were holding on to. The elephant in our family room had never seemed bigger than how it looked from where I was sitting in my mother's car.

But I realized that I couldn't keep on living with this large animal, and I was tired of stepping around it. I felt like something had to give. I didn't know precisely what to do but was smart enough to realize that what I had been doing for the past few years hadn't worked. Before I made this trip, I had known that I wanted to see Margaret, but I couldn't face another family gathering with the firebomb of my sister's autism igniting again the pages of the family history. I'd thought anything had to be better than that. So I took a deep breath, picked up the phone, and called Margaret to ask if she wanted to go out for lunch with me, alone. After a few seconds of mutual anxiety-ridden silence, she mumbled yes and hung up on me.

Standing there with the phone in my hand, listening to the dial tone, I had let my thoughts run through the minefield of things that might go wrong during a lunch date with Margaret. I thought it all through. I surrendered myself to whatever might happen and wrote it down on my calendar: "Pick up Margaret for lunch, 11:45 AM, Friday." And then I went to the liquor cabinet and poured myself a stiff drink.

I grew up alongside my sister's eccentricities, never really noticing how strange she could be, because I'd never known anything else. Just as I always knew to jump in the air to avoid being shocked by the shorted-out refrigerator at the lake house, and to move the cat out of the fruit basket before putting the bananas in it, I always knew that with Margaret along we were likely to be the center of attention at any public event, and not in a good way. When Margaret misbehaved, everyone would stare, and I always thought they were looking at me, too. Sometimes the faces were just curious; sometimes they were angry or afraid. After a while I felt like people were staring even when they weren't. As we grew older and I passed her developmentally, I began to feel responsible for the staring.

It was confusing, at best, to be learning life's rules and social graces alongside someone who consistently violated every one of them. We wandered through an etiquette desert without a guide. We needed an Emily Post of autism to lead us through the rough patches, but when she didn't show up we forged ahead anyway. My siblings and I remain, as adults, a self-guided lot, still figuring things out as we go.

I often feel like this about my life: mapless, guideless, as if I am actually hammering the nails into the wood of the bridge I need to walk across one crappy, ramshackle board at a time. I always feel like I'm showing up just a bit unprepared in life, like everyone else got the memo or took the class while I was busy looking for someplace to park or finding the bathroom. I thought about that now as I sat outside Margaret's house, trying to work up enough surrender to get out of the car and knock on the door.

Sitting in the car, I reminded myself that lunch was a

fairly safe option. Everybody has to eat, right? So I sent a prayer to the Universe to help everything be okay. I prayed for optimism and grace. I wished I could have a drink, but it wasn't even noon yet. Instead, I opened the door and got out of the car.

2.

lunch date

Eating in fast food restaurants seldom requires more than everyday good manners.

—*On Dining Out*, EMILY POST'S ETIQUETTE

a S AN ADULT with severe autism, my sister has had her share of struggles. Thankfully, I recalled as I stood next to the car, housing is no longer one of them. Margaret lives in an old Craftsman-style house near Gonzaga University in Spokane. My parents bought and renovated the house when it became clear that the crappy public housing apartments available to Margaret weren't going to cut it. She kept getting kicked out. "Too noisy," the landlords always said. *Well, duh!* I always thought. Anyone who has ever lived in one of those shaky, 1970s-era cardboard constructions will tell you that you can hear someone opening a box of Kleenex three doors down.

So imagine what might happen if you lived next door to someone who weighed 180 pounds and was in the habit of throwing herself against the walls and floors during occasional periods of frustration. Too noisy.

So Margaret's house became a group home for adults with disabilities expressly because the landlords, my parents, would never kick Margaret out. It has been home to Margaret and her three housemates for many years. A twenty-four-hour staff supports the four of them in living as independently as they can. I painted the house one summer right before Margaret moved in, and I loved every corner. It's the kind of house everyone should have—a big porch and a nice yard, lots of windows to let in the sunshine. The neighborhood sidewalks end in rounded curbs, and the streets—wide enough to drive a circus through—are lined with lovely old trees.

From where I was standing at the curb now, I could see groups of college students heading to campus in their cargo shorts and backpacks. On the way there I'd driven past a herd of toddlers being shepherded along by a couple of middle-aged women. The air was full of chattering little voices and a rainbow of T-shirts as bright as the summer flowers. It made me happy to see the "neighborhoodiness" of Margaret's neighborhood, especially when I remembered that some of the neighbors in the other nice, big houses initially weren't too keen on the idea of having a group home in their midst.

I looked at Margaret's front door, knowing I was right on time. Punctuality is a family affliction. We are the people who are eight and half minutes early when the rest of America is running fifteen minutes late. I also knew that Margaret had probably been waiting restlessly for hours, possibly because she was excited to see me but mostly because she was just anxious. We are indeed an anxious people; we like to stick to the schedule, get on with the show. Margaret's disorder seems to amplify that characteristic. From the curb, I could see her standing at the picture window in the living room watching me. Even so, she actually let me come up the walkway instead of running out the door, pulling her coat on. She let me climb the stairs and knock on the door like a normal person, which was fun for me.

Normally she might just charge out the door when she saw the car coming down the street, and I'd miss out on practicing the normalcy of it all—the walkway, the knock, the door, the greeting, the introductions and small talk, the leave-taking. Even now, as an adult, I loved the distinct phases of events that I had missed out on in my youth, the almost invisible transitions in social situations. I even loved the moments of awkwardness when nobody knew what to do next. I had spent so many years under the steamroller of autism that these bumps and breaks still held a great deal of appeal for me. These adult days followed a childhood during which greetings and partings meant chasing my mother, who was chasing my sister, who was running through a crowd at some church or school function, and I would wave hello or good-bye at people who gaped at us as we sprinted past.

Now, when I knocked, Margaret yanked the door open. "Hi, Eileen!" she said, waving at me from just two feet away and holding the door open. It was almost like we were regular people. Uninvited, because Margaret wouldn't think to invite someone in, I stepped across the threshold to greet my sister. *Here is Margaret, in my arms, the real person.* She allowed me a brief hug and then scurried off to get her things. I turned to greet the staff member who'd come in from the living room. Two of Margaret's housemates crowded into the foyer to see who was at the door, and I said hello to them, too.

Sarah is the resident busybody at the house. My parents tell me that she makes it her job to keep tabs on Margaret, Ken, Gerald, and the staff—their comings and goings, as well as their smallest tragedies and victories. It's nearly impossible to keep a secret when Sarah is around, as she is so diligent in her information gathering. "Where you goin'?" she now demanded of me, and I began to understand where she got her reputation. I told her we were going out to lunch. In exchange for this piece of information she offered me some from her own stash: Margaret had gone to my parents' house a few days earlier. Then my mother brought Margaret home. And her boots were in the closet, too. She told me all of this rapidly and ended with a satisfied nod. Ken didn't say anything. He just fluttered his hand at me when I asked him how he was doing and grimaced in an attempt to smile.

During this exchange of niceties, Margaret was a tempest of activity. She grabbed her fanny pack off the table by the door, heaved it around her hips, and clicked the clasp shut. Then she rushed over to Sarah, who bowed her head so that Margaret could smell her hair, an old habit of my sister's. Margaret gave a big sniff, yelled, "Bye, Sarah!" and trotted out the door and down the wooden steps of the big blue house, ignoring everyone else. I'd forgotten how fast she could move, so I was doing double time trying to keep up as I called good-bye to the rest of them over my shoulder and followed her out to the car. So much for transitions. So much for leaving behind greetings and partings while running.

Margaret stood and waited for me next to the car, her hands clasped in front of her and resting on her big tummy, her eyes cast down at her feet. I looked her over as I walked toward the car, thinking that in her tennis shoes, blue jeans, and pastel Windbreaker, my older sister looked like any other thirty-something woman on her day off. Her short hair looked good, turning reddish in the summer sunlight. I noticed that she was showing some gray, but at least her hair didn't look like she had recently tried to cut it herself, a longtime favorite prank.

When we were younger, if Margaret got her hands on a pair of scissors, she would go looking for my mother. Then she'd grab a hank of her hair and call out sweetly, "Hi, Mom!" When my mother looked up from whatever she was doing, Margaret would chirp, "You don't cut your hair, Mom!" Snip! And then my mother, too late, would yell, "Margaret! Don't cut your hair!" And my sister would laugh and laugh and run away with her crazy new haircut.

I didn't know how often she was cutting her hair these days. But it was still pretty hard to find a pair of scissors around my parents' house. The last time I had been home for Christmas, I'd found myself folding, licking, and tearing wrapping paper to cover my presents, because the scissors had been hidden so well that no one could remember where they were. This was just one example of how we tried to anticipate Margaret's behavior and not only failed but also made things harder on ourselves. Even better, Margaret probably knew where the scissors were and could have saved me some time and saliva if I'd just asked her to get them for me.

My family had spent a collective lifetime trying to predict what Margaret might do and how to deal with it. But she was as mutable as a summer storm—and as surprising and terrifying. Funny haircuts were just the tip of the iceberg, and not so important. The more significant and overwhelming issue was our inability to connect with her, to know for sure if we were reaching the person who was Margaret behind the disorder that was autism, and what, in the end, we were supposed to do about it. Sometimes we had to be satisfied with smaller accomplishments, like her haircut. The fact that she had left it alone was a signal to me that she was feeling okay inside. Besides, her haircut also looked really cute, which made me happy. I've always hoped my sister could have a normal life, as far as that is possible. And when she looks like everyone else, she blends in more easily.

Margaret rubbed her chin as she waited for me to cross the lawn and unlock the car. She didn't look at me as she yanked the door open, jumped in, and slammed it shut so hard that the car rocked from side to side. I'd forgotten about this behavior, so it startled me for a minute. I don't know what it is with Margaret and doors, but "closed" to her always takes this much force—no more, no less. As the rocking stopped, I got in. She reached over her shoulder and yanked on her seat belt. She waited until I turned the key, then she leaned over, released the emergency brake, and shifted the car into drive for me. "Thanks," I said, surprised. But she didn't say anything, just waited for me to drive and looked out the window as we made our way to the local diner. It was a short drive, and neither of us spoke on the way there. As soon as I eased into a parking space, Margaret reached over and threw the car into park, yanked up on the emergency brake, turned the car off, and tossed me the keys. Then she undid her seat belt and jumped out of the car in one motion, slamming the door just as hard as when she had gotten in. She speed-walked toward the diner, and I laughed out loud, even as I hurried to follow her. This was new. U-Park Valet Service.

Arnie's was probably packed with Gonzaga University students during the school year, but on this summer day the 1950s-style diner was empty but for us and the staff—two young women wearing chest-hugging T-shirts and tight blue jeans. From what I gathered, one of them, the cook, was terribly hungover. It was a little worrying to think about ordering lunch knowing that it was to be prepared by the person who kept leaving her post to lie down in a booth and moan. But I tried to be brave, and we took our seats at the counter to look over the menu.

As we sat on our red vinyl stools, I found myself feeling smug. *Here we are. Two sisters having lunch. How nice. How normal. What's so hard about this?* In truth, I'd been dreading this lunch date all week. But by the time we got our butts onto the shiny red stools, I was cautiously optimistic and feeling a little giddy with the success of getting to the restaurant without mishap. Margaret's routine had been interrupted, and she was okay and seemed happy to be with me. That this feeling was short-lived didn't make it any less sweet.

Margaret quickly ordered and drank a couple of Cokes. I tried to make small talk—you know, like you would when you are having lunch with your sister. It seemed like the normal thing to do, but then again, I'd been away from home so long that I tended to get my "normals" mixed up. I started asking her about what she had been doing lately. I knew she was training for the Washington State Special Olympics swimming competition, which meant she was spending a lot of time at the pool with her team and her coach. Although she loves to swim, she does not like to talk about swimming. She doesn't like to talk much, period. And when Margaret is not in the mood to talk, she responds like she's blindfolded and handcuffed, sitting under the harsh glare of a bare bulb in an interrogation room. Of course, I tried to converse with her anyway.

"Did you go to swimming practice this week?"

Silence.

"Margs, did you go to swimming practice this week?"

"Yes!" she barked, not looking at me.

"Who else was there?"

Silence.

"Margs, who else was at swimming practice with you?"

"Yes! You went to swimming practice!"

She gets her pronouns mixed up, which is not uncommon for someone with autism. She often says "you" when she means "I," but I usually know what she is talking about. This time there was no ambiguity. She was saying, "Shut the fuck up and let me drink my Coke, for Chrissakes!" But I kept on trying, like an idiot.

"I like your haircut, Margs," I said. "Who cut your hair? Did Sherry cut it?"

My mother, grandmother, and Margaret have all been getting their hair cut by Sherry for the last twenty-five years or so, and Margaret loves Sherry, but she didn't bite. Instead, she swiveled her stool to the right, away from me, as if to say, "If I can't see you, maybe you will go away!" I finally took the hint and shut up. I didn't want to piss her off, because she might try to leave. Really. At that moment, I wouldn't have been surprised to see her get up and run out the door as if to say, "I've had enough of this crap!" I didn't want her to feel like she had to leave. I also didn't want her to have to defend her silence by chucking something across the room, like the stainless-steel napkin dispenser in front of us, or the ketchup bottle, or my water glass. I scanned the counter in front of us, imagining the possibilities.

What am I doing, anyway? I asked myself. *Who is this chatty conversation for?* She obviously didn't want to talk, and I wasn't going to get any information from her. She clearly didn't want any from me. Maybe I was trying to make us seem more normal for the hungover café staff.

As stupid as that sounds, it's probably the truth. I spent the first half of my life painfully self-conscious about what people thought of us and wanting to seem more normal. And here I was doing it again, thinking that we must look weird, that two grown women in their thirties don't usually sit next to each other in complete silence at a café. Unless they are fighting. Or really hungover. But I'd also been thinking a lot about giving up on "usually" and "normal," so I shut up and just sat there drinking my Coke.

Perched on her stool, Margaret seemed happy and quiet after I finally stopped talking to her. She spread the fingers of her right hand and laid them out on the counter in front of her. She pressed all five digits into the Formica, then subtracted one so that she was pressing four, then three, then two, then the thumb went and there was just the index finger. Then she added them back in: one, two, three, four, five. She chuckled to herself as she did it again.

We sat. The griddle popped and spat grease. The fry basket gurgled, the cook moaned, the soda fountain kicked out Margaret's third Coke. Campy music poured out of small speakers mounted around the room. The fan whirred overhead.

"Hi, Eileen," Margaret said brightly after a while, as if we had not been sitting there in silence for ten minutes.

"Hi, Margs," I said calmly, as if I had not just traveled sixteen hundred miles to take her out to lunch.

"Hi," she said.

"Hi, Margs," I said.

Another silent minute passed.

"That's Bobby Darrin," she said.

And sure enough, when I paused to listen, the buttery tones of Bobby Darrin came crooning out of the corner speaker. Just one file of the thousands in my sister's mental archive of musicians and lyrics that spans decades. I remembered back when she was our house DJ, spinning records during all waking hours, forming the soundtrack of our childhood. Bobby Darrin was a favorite, as were the songs from *Jesus Christ Superstar,* Arthur Fiedler's Boston Pops, and the Electric Light Orchestra. One might hear "Hold on Tight to Your Dreams" on the heels of "What's the Buzz" or "I'm Coming to Get You in a Taxi, Honey."

"Yes, that's right, Margs. That's Bobby Darrin."

"That's Bobby Darrin, Eileen."

"Yep. That's Bobby Darrin, Margs."

We listened together. *"Oh, Louie Miller, he disappeared,*

babe! After drawin' out all his hard-earned cash. And now MacHeath spends just like a sailor. Could it be our boy's done something rash?"

"Bobby Darrin," Margaret whispered to herself and laughed quietly.

Then all of a sudden she said, "Hi, there!" and she smiled at me. Right at me. Not looking sideways and then yanking her eyes back down to the counter like before. Her lovely hazel eyes looked right into my face. She smiled, as if welcoming me. "Hi, Eileen!" she said, like I'd just arrived, like I'd just pulled up in front of her house after she had not seen me in ages. "Hi, there, Eileen!" Like it was Christmas morning.

I didn't say anything, even though I felt like I might weep. I just smiled at her. I hummed a few bars of "Mack the Knife." Still smiling, Margaret went back to the finger-pressing game, now alternating hands.

"Do you want another Coke?"

This question came from the server behind the counter, the one who was not supine in the corner. She must have been about twenty. Her long brunette hair was pulled back in a ponytail, out of her wide-set eyes and pretty face. She was tough, way too cool to be friendly. But I realized that when she asked this question, she was not asking me. She was looking at my sister. She was asking Margaret. For this, I suddenly loved her, this complete stranger.

Often as soon as people pick up on Margaret's weirdo vibe, they start directing their questions at whoever is with her. "Does she want French fries?" they'll ask me nervously, glancing at her. "Does she bite?" they might as well be asking. They mean well. They're just trying to get the food on the table. It throws off a server's game when she tries to hand out a pair of menus and a customer shouts "No!" and shoves a menu back at her.

Our waitress was smarter than most. When that had happened earlier, she just took a step back and then removed the offending menu without saying anything, letting us both order from mine. But here she was again, trying to treat my sister like a normal person.

"Do you want another Coke?" she asked again, and waited. After a second, Margaret glanced up from the counter and said, "Yes!" She took one last slurp on her straw before shoving the glass across the counter.

"Thanks," I said as the young woman delivered the glass back across the counter. "What do you want to say, Margs?"

"Thank you!" my sister said, as she grabbed the still-fizzing glass out of the young woman's hand, slammed it down in front of her, and took a noisy pull on the straw.

The young woman flicked her eyes at me, and the corners of her mouth jerked upward in a kind of smile. *Maybe she understands that this is just how Margaret moves,* I thought. Margaret shoves, yanks, slams, jerks, runs, and throws herself in and out of chairs and cars. It's nothing personal. She'll try to slow down if you remind her, but it just makes her nervous to try to do things at someone else's pace.

We sat in peaceful silence until the food arrived. I looked up in anticipation. The young woman smiled back at me as she set down my plate with a clunk. Then she tried to set down Margaret's. My sister looked horrified. "No!" she cried, and pushed the plate away with a forceful hand. "No!" The big dinner plate was heaped with food, and because it was so heavy, the young woman kept trying to set it down. But Margaret was playing defense and her voice got louder. "No-eeeeee!" She shoved the plate away again. This time the server almost dropped it. I reached over and grabbed the plate and set it down next to me.

"Got it," I said.

The young woman stood there for a second staring at us like she was trying to figure out what she had done wrong. She looked down at the steaming plate, loaded with a hearty chicken sandwich and French fries, trying to determine the source of my sister's horror. I was puzzled, too.

"Don't you want your sandwich?" I asked Margaret.

"NothankyouEileen!" she said in one breath, staring at the counter. She sounded panicked.

"Maybe later," I said to the waitress, so that she would know it wasn't her fault. She started to smile. But then Margaret gave the plate another shove. "NO!" The smile disappeared and the server backed away from us. I moved the plate over to the left of me, out of Margaret's reach, feeling depressed. Forget about making polite conversation. If we couldn't even manage to have lunch together like normal people, what in the hell was I supposed to do with her? How was I supposed to be part of her life? Maybe I should just give up this experiment and stay away. Margaret glanced at the plate on the far side of me with menace.

Why? Why? I didn't know, and worse, she couldn't tell me. It would seem reasonable to assume that if you ordered food at a diner it would probably show up in front of you. It also seemed reasonable that, in ordering it, you implied that you wanted to eat it. But my reasoning skills often backfired when I was trying to figure out what my sister wanted or needed. I would even go so far as to say that most of the time I didn't understand what my sister was thinking, and every time I failed, I felt my heart break a little more. Or maybe I should say I felt the heartbreak I continue to have, because it's been this way for a very long time. This is the chasm between us, a great, yawning disconnect that neither one of us can breach. But if it felt shitty, it also felt familiar, which was some kind of cold comfort.

THIS WAS HOW I had felt on our bike ride the year before during my spring break from grad school. I'd thought it would be a sure thing, something we could do together that she would really enjoy. Half a mile from the house, Margaret had stopped her bike and stood over it, bawling. She just cried and cried without making any noise, which I somehow hated even more than her screaming. Every once in a while she would lift up her

T-shirt and wipe her streaming face. I just stood there feeling helpless, her sadness a physical weight on my chest as I watched her silent and terrible sorrow. I knew I couldn't do anything to help, but I tried anyway, feeling useless, like I often did.

"What's the matter, Margaret?" I asked.

"You're crying!"

"Why are you crying?"

"You're sad," she said, trying to give me an answer.

"Why are you sad?"

"Hi, Eileen!" she said to me, smiling through her tears.

"Do you want to go back to the house?" I asked.

"No!"

"Do you want to go for a bike ride?"

Silence.

This is what it feels like to be unable to comfort your family, people so close to you genetically. It seems a given that you should be able to reach each other in this most basic way. But nothing I did seemed to make a difference in moments like these.

So we sat there for a while with the wind in our faces. It started to rain a little bit, but we just stood there. We kept our hands on the handlebars and our feet on the pavement, standing on the pedestrian overpass down by the Spokane River. After a while, Margaret took a deep breath, exhaled, wiped her eyes on her sleeve, and rode on without saying anything. Later, when we got back to the house and one of the staff members asked if we'd had a good time, Margaret's answer was unequivocal: "Yes!"

• • •

So as we sat there on our stools, I didn't know what to say, as usual. But I was learning what to do. Wait. Shut up. Wait some more. Be kind by being quiet. I couldn't fix my sister. And as much as I wanted to, I usually couldn't make her feel better. But I could sit with her in her sorrow, in her silence, with her cooling chicken sandwich, in her struggle to allow me to invade her routine so that I could be a part of her life.

In the spirit of shutting up and waiting, I finished my lunch in silence while Margaret finished her final Coke. About the time I finished eating, the cook groaned, rolled over, and went outside to smoke a cigarette. I got a box for Margaret's food and paid the bill. "Thanks," I said to our server, who had recovered her composure and was able to act like it was perfectly normal to order food, try to throw it behind the counter, let it get cold, and then take it in a to-go box. "No problem," she said.

"Are you ready to go?" I asked my big sister. These words were like some kind of abracadabra. Margaret jumped down from her stool, grabbed her fanny pack, sucked in her tummy, threw the straps around her waist, and snapped the clasp shut. Then she headed for the door at full tilt. But when she got there she stopped abruptly and turned. She looked directly at the young woman behind the counter and broke into a radiant smile.

"Okay! G-bye! Thank you very much for the lunch! Haveaniceday! G-bye!"

Margaret shouted this in one breath, all the time smiling

and waving madly. The young woman smiled a real smile and waved back, shyly, uncertain under the weight of such gratitude. Suddenly she was beautiful, her face reflecting my sister's strange and simple joy. "You're welcome," she said.

She got it right, Margaret, some of the time, anyway. She knew she was supposed to say thank you for food and hospitality even if she didn't appear to accept them. Besides, most of us don't get it right all of the time, do we?

And that helped me, seeing someone else understand Margaret for a minute, recognizing her attempt to sustain a normal exchange, however brief, seeing the kindness that strangers are capable of. Maybe it's not so complicated. We might not ever be like normal sisters, but what does that mean anyway?

My whole life with Margaret I'd always felt like we were in a hurry. But now I wanted to think I was trying to learn to follow her at my own pace and let her go at her own. So when we first got to Arnie's and she raced across the parking lot, her pink and purple Windbreaker flapping in the breeze, I followed behind and made sure to watch for cars. But I didn't chase her. And I didn't try to get her to slow down. I let her go in and be the first one through the door of the café, ringing the bells over the door with a bit more force than they were probably used to. I let her go in, knowing that she might just stand there and stare if someone asked her a question and that people might feel awkward when she didn't answer. It's that thing about transitions; they aren't always smooth, but they have to happen if you want to leave the place you are and get to another. I let her go. I just let her go. I was beginning to realize that her life was her own, and that I was no parachute.

Margaret slammed the door behind her, and the bells jangled. I was right on her tail as she raced toward the car. The wind ruffled her short hair and caught her Wind-breaker, making it billow like a kite. She grinned at me over the top of the car as she waited for me to unlock the door so that she could get in and turn the key for me. As I smiled back, I thought, *There might be hope for us after all.*

3.

let her eat cake

The good guest is almost invisible, enjoying him- or herself,
communing with fellow guests, and, most of all, enjoying the
generous hospitality of the hosts.

—*On Wedding Guests,* EMILY POST'S ETIQUETTE

THE SUMMER OF the chicken sandwich ended. After my visit, I flew back to New Mexico, said good-bye to my friends, packed up my things, and drove a quaking U-Haul from south to north with one nervous dog, two angry cats, and my spouse, Brendan, who insisted on playing his guitar in the truck cab, so I had to drive for thirteen hundred miles with one hand guarding the right side of my head. Now we all lived in Oregon, a mere five hours from my childhood home. I was nearer to the family tree, but not much closer to figuring out what I was supposed to do about Margaret.

She was on my mind a lot that first year, even at the

most unlikely times, like when I was supposed to be working. Jobs were scarce in the beautiful little tourist town I moved to, so I took any kind of work I could get, including teaching English to migrant fruit pickers and working in a brownie factory, although I was trained for neither. I also wrote some stories for the local newspaper. They asked me to do a couple of features for the bridal guide, the kind of pieces that the regular staff would refuse to do, the kind of story I had balked at when I was a salaried newspaper person myself. But as the new freelancer in town, I was grateful to be working at all. So I knew I should be paying attention to my assignment instead of letting my mind wander to my big sister. But I just couldn't help myself. She ran amok in my imagination, just as she had in my life.

As I worked my way through the interviews for the bridal stories, one wedding planner made a really big impression on me with her kind of no-bullshit approach to putting on the Big White Dress Show. She was very tall, blonde, and had that kind of Germanic competence that made me believe she was capable of just about anything. If the bridal party got caught in traffic, she could pick up the limo with one hand and wade to safety. That's the impression Teresa made. Maybe that's why I found myself dying to ask her the most inappropriate questions during our interview.

The topic of my story was second weddings, and we had kind of wandered into the territory of difficult relatives. I found myself wanting to ask, "So what would you do, then, after seating the ex-stepmother-in-law of the bride, I mean, and somebody started, I don't know, running around the church and singing or something? Or what if somebody started laughing really hard during the vows? A guest, I mean. An adult. How would you handle that?"

I really did want to know the answers. Teresa seemed like she might be the one person who could help me sort out what had happened in my own past. Hashing things out with her might be a kind of bridal morbidity and mortality session, like what hospitals have to assess why people died. Although it wouldn't change what had already happened, I was comforted by the thought that somebody else might have known how to handle things. In the end, however, I figured this line of questioning could kill the flow of the interview, so I didn't ask.

I thought about my own wedding, years before. It was hard to believe that I was no longer in my twenties, but back then it was harder for me to believe that I'd ever get married at all. I was shocked by the fact that I liked anyone enough to spend seven days a week with him without wanting to do him bodily harm. I'm not the most patient person, and this was, after all, a man who borrowed my toothbrush, lost my apartment keys, frequently stepped on me as he was crossing a room, elbowed me in the face every time he put on his seat belt, locked me out of the apartment for hours at a time, or, alternatively, left my apartment door wide open when he left so that any of the junkies in my building could have let themselves in to make a sandwich or smoke some crack. This was Brendan—generally an hour late for everything while I was fifteen minutes early. Somehow, it seemed, we belonged together.

Like many young people, I hadn't given much thought to the marriage part of things. I figured that would take care of itself. I had more important things on my mind. I was worried about the wedding, the cake, my sister, and her autism. And not necessarily in that order.

MARGARET WOULD APPEAR to love weddings. She shows great enthusiasm whenever the topic comes up. But the truth is, Margaret loves wedding *cake*. To her, the entire affair—the invitations, the fancy clothes, the sacred vows, the touching family photos, the lavish banquet, the general hullabaloo—is meaningless, tiresome filler. She focuses her energies completely upon that magic moment during the reception when the lovely couple finally cuts the goddamn cake and lets everyone else have a piece. Nothing wrong with that, is there? The trouble is, everything that happens before the fork hits the plate doesn't interest her much. It's downtime, really. A tedious waiting period most often filled, depending on her mood, with laughter or tears, and not the quiet, happy, wedding kind.

When we were growing up, I don't recall that Margaret made a scene at anyone's wedding reception. Which isn't to claim that she didn't make any memorable fuss. It's just that by that point in the evening she had so much competition that it's likely any outburst might have gone unnoticed. Irish Catholic receptions are really just one big scene, after all—a big drinking, fighting, dancing scene. More than once I heard my grandmother say on the way to the car after one of these high-energy, boozy affairs, "Oh, wasn't that lovely! And nobody fell down." Her parents owned a tavern after (and during) Prohibition, which is one reason she didn't drink until she was almost seventy; this woman has seen it all, so she knows what she is talking about.

But wedding ceremonies, even for rowdy Irish Catholics like us, are supposed to be different. The marriage rites are generally a time of quiet and reverence, a time to focus on the sacred union between two people who have chosen to (try to) spend (they hope) the rest of their lives together.

Weddings can range widely within an acceptable scope of good taste—religious versus secular, indoor or outdoor, tuxes and silk as opposed to beach attire are just a few types that come to mind. However, I can say with some certainty that most marriage ceremonies don't include a rousing, hand-clapping solo of "I've Been Workin' on the Railroad" from one of the guests. I was almost a teenager before I realized that this kind of musical interlude was not common at nuptial services. No, in fact, this kind of thing was actually viewed as a disruption, the kind engineered by my sister Margaret.

Margaret's particular solo went something like this: "Someone's in *(clap)* the kitchen *(clap)* with Di *(clap)* NAH!

(clap clap) Someone's in *(clap)* the kitchen *(clap)* I know-oh-oh-oh!" and concluded with a resounding, "Ha! Ha! Ha! You be quiet, Margaret!" as my sister scolded herself loudly at the end of the verse.

Sometimes such an outburst would include a game of tag, with my mother being "It." This game often drew withering looks from the officiating priest as my chortling sister ran up the aisle and around the altar with my silent, grim-faced mother in hot pursuit. How often I watched my big sister Margaret sprinting around the Eucharistic minister, or rocking from side to side in her wide-leg stance up on the altar, clapping and singing. Sometimes she'd just start laughing during a quiet part of the service, or scold herself in a parroting of our mother's voice. "Margaret, now you behave! Now you be quiet!" Her voice seemed to echo endlessly across the cool, quiet sanctuary. Or perhaps when my mother whispered in her ear ("Margaret, you have to be quiet or we have to leave"), we'd hear only Margaret's side of the conversation, as if she were on the phone. "No! Okay! That's good behaving, Mom!" I'd sink down in the pew, thankful that it was always pretty dark in Sacred Heart Catholic Church, hoping people would think it was somebody else's family making all the noise.

These episodes all ended the same way: my gentle mother wordlessly hauled Margaret, who was either wailing or laughing, down the aisle and to the back of the church as half of the congregation turned to watch while the other half pretended that nothing was happening. The doors at the back of the church would bang shut behind them, heads would swivel back to the priest, and then the service would continue.

I actually can't remember a wedding service in my childhood that Margaret did *not* contribute to in some very memorable way. Maybe that's because if she'd behaved herself, I wouldn't have had anything to remember. The celebrations I do recall are absolutely burned into my memory. As I write this, I can still feel the frozen stare of a bride and groom, family friends, as the entire congregation turned to look at the Garvins. It was 1978. The groom's eyes were wider than his tie. The bride craned her veil-covered head over one puffy satin and lace shoulder pad to try to locate the source of an undeniable and unbelievable ruckus from our pew. I don't remember what Margaret had done. Only that it was so loud that even the priest couldn't ignore it and had paused in the middle of the ceremony to look our way.

This was my chance to smile and give a little wave. "Hi, Jim! Hi, Jane! Oh, good, they saw me. Now they know we're here," I said to my eight-year-old self, not realizing that most weddings were not meant to be interactive.

This is how it went through the marriages of our cousins, family friends, and second cousins. And at some point we'd usually get to share the spotlight when Margaret performed her routine, always unique and never predictable. Suffice it to say people never had to say, years later, "Did the Garvins come to our wedding? I just can't remember." They always remembered.

THINKING BACK ON all this as I wrote my bridal stories, it struck me that we could have used someone like Teresa, not so much as a wedding planner but as a kind of crisis manager. Perhaps Teresa could have been our Emily Post of autism, the person to smooth out the crazy in our lives and make things seem more normal. This woman handled inclement weather, ill-behaved relatives, and emotional meltdowns without getting a hair out of place. Months after I interviewed her for my wedding feature, I read about her in the news section of our little paper when she pulled off one of the most heroic wedding rescues I've ever heard of. When a wildfire drove one wedding party from their site, she rushed over to another wedding she was managing on the same day at a different location and convinced the other bride to let the first couple come on over and share the same reception area—*all this as the bride was marching down the aisle.* When I read that story, I thought, "Man, she is tough!" But when all was said and done, I still didn't think Teresa would have been any match for Margaret.

When my siblings and I got married, my sister's history as Most Memorable Guest gave us some pause. I wasn't the only one asking myself, "What should I do about Margaret?" Over the years the question weighed heavily on each of us as we, by turns, got engaged and planned the Big Day. Our oldest sister, Ann, tested the waters first, marrying her college sweetheart, Rob, when she was just twenty-one. Being the oldest, her instincts were untested and kind of screwed up, so she asked Margaret and me to be bridesmaids along with her best girlfriends, Bridget and Lori. Maybe if she had been older, or if she hadn't been the first lemming over the ledge, she might have been too smart to ask either of us. I don't know which was the more foolish choice—the sixteen-year-old who got superdrunk and threw up in the parking lot at the reception behind her boyfriend's van (me) or the nineteen-year-old autistic sister who threw such a fit before the ceremony even began that our mother nearly missed the wedding (Margaret).

The problem, of course, was the cake.

The trouble began early one chilly afternoon a few days before Christmas in 1986. We'd all gathered at St. Aloysius Church with the groom's parents and his five siblings for a couple of hours of pre-wedding torture known as Wedding Photo Time. The idea was to get the pictures out of the way early in order to enjoy an afternoon ceremony and evening reception. It was a simple misunderstanding, really. Margaret thought she would get wedding cake after the wedding photos were over. She did not understand that the pictures came first, and then we sat around in scratchy taffeta, freezing our asses off in the unheated church basement in the middle of winter, waiting for the wedding to start. Then came the two-hour ceremony in a frigid, cavernous church. After

that we went to the reception and went through the niceties of the receiving line, heartfelt speeches, and special
dances. THEN came the cake. This was just too much
information for my sister; I've come to believe that it's
too much information for anybody, really.

As this miscommunication unfolded, we were about in
the middle of the grueling picture-taking process. There
we were, seven Garvins and eight Modarellis in our new
shoes and nice clothes being poked and prodded and repo-
sitioned by the grouchy photographer, who was wearing
way too much Old Spice. Our families barely knew each
other, and here we all were, crowded shoulder to shoulder, just hours before the ceremony that would clinch the
lifelong union of the oldest children. It was awkward, but
just in that regular wedding way. The tension mounted to
an irregular level when it became clear that Margaret was
winding herself up for a supreme blowout.

She made it through the pictures with a few tears here
and there, asking where in the hell the cake was. And
then she simply came undone, throwing herself on the
floor of the church, kicking and screaming in her beautiful maroon taffeta dress that our mother had stitched
by hand. "You want cake and punch! You want cake
and punch! Cake! And! Punch! Nooooooooo!" She rolled
around on the floor in front of everyone, banging the
sturdy plastic handle of her bridesmaid's bouquet at our
feet. "Noooooooooo! You want CAKE AND PUNCH!
Ahhhhhhhhhhh! Nooooooooooooooooooo!"

This was pretty much what my brothers and I had been waiting for all day; we knew it was just a matter of time before Margaret lost her grip. But I will never forget the silent horror on the Modarelli kids' faces. I mean, who yells in church? Who pounds her dyed-to-match satin pumps against the marble altar steps? Who kicks and screams and throws her legs over her head so you can see the white crotch of her pantyhose? My sister, that's who.

When it became clear that she was not going to calm down in the next half hour, let alone make it through the service, my mother announced that she would take Margaret home, and nearly missed the wedding of her firstborn. Happily, a kind friend of Ann's stepped up and volunteered to take Margaret to her place and hang out with her until the wedding was over. Meg somehow managed to coax Margaret out of the church and into her car. The rest of us started breathing again, pulled ourselves together, and soldiered on, because that's what you do at a wedding. Ann and Rob suffered the minor awkwardness of having an extra groomsman at the altar, but I doubt anyone even remembers that.

In later years, I couldn't remember if Margaret actually made it to the reception, because I had been too busy getting drunk in preparation for my big throw-up scene. So I recently asked Ann, and she confirmed that Margaret had, in fact, made it to the party. "Oh, yes. Yes, she did. She had CAKE! AND! PUNCH! Mom said she had such a good time that her nylons were in shreds by the time she got home," Ann said, adding "I have no idea what that means."

BY THE TIME I got married, twelve years later, I'd had a lot of time to think about what to do about Margaret. I knew that I had to approach this situation assuming that something would probably go wrong, and with great gusto. But I wanted Margaret to come, and that was just fine with Brendan, who was so overwhelmed with the complications of planning a wedding that he just said yes to everything and then left the country for two months. However, in an attempt to learn from history, I thought it might be useful to decrease my mother's status as a flight risk. So I suggested that one of the staff members who worked at Margaret's group home come along and be her date. That suited everybody just fine.

Felicia drove Margaret to Seattle from Spokane and the two of them shared a motel room at the same place everyone else was staying. Felicia brought my big sister to a party we had the day before we got married, and the two of them did some sightseeing on their own. They even came together to an impromptu ladies-only breakfast the day of the wedding, and because Felicia was in charge of Margaret, I got to visit with my mother and Ann without worrying about which one of us was going to have to leave the table and deal with Margaret if she decided to chuck her French toast across the table at a cousin or bridesmaid.

During the wedding itself, I didn't hear Margaret at

all. She sat quietly with her date, looking pretty in a pale yellow dress with small red flowers on it. Then again, there was quite a ruckus going on anyway, so I might not have noticed if she was being noisy. First of all, Brendan and I got married on an antique ferryboat on Lake Union in Seattle, and the regular boat traffic was going by during the ceremony. We had recruited a large yellow Labrador retriever named Honey to bear the rings, and the dog was so excited by all the people and the smells that she kind of detoured around for a while, attempting to greet everybody, and had to be coaxed back to her job. The amateur bagpipers, whom we hadn't really screened very well, seemed to have trouble getting started at the same time and wheezed along jerkily as we marched down the aisle. At one point there was a spontaneous a cappella performance from the Balkan men's quartet from our soccer team, who showed up in their eye-catching skirts.

Also, we couldn't get our unity candle to light for several long minutes, which caused a lot of nervous laughter. When we finally did get the damn thing lit, Brendan was so relieved that he put down his still-burning taper and nearly set fire to the fancy tablecloth under the candle. Then he snatched up the taper and blew it out, extinguishing the unity candle all over again. Our kind and exasperated minister pushed us out of the way and whipped out one of those huge plastic barbecue lighters, which she used to relight our wick. I try not to think about the symbolism of this part of the ceremony and its possible spiritual implications for our marriage. The point is that it is possible I just didn't notice any outburst from my sister. I had reconciled myself to some kind of Margaret-sized contribution, but I didn't hear a peep.

When it came time to cut the cake, however, I did notice a big, adult-sized finger swipe in the frosting on the front of it, but no one else saw it, and I just moved a flower to cover it up. Our friends and family gathered around the cake table listening to toasts, and Margaret hovered at the edge of the crowd, nervously twisting her fingers but waiting patiently for us to get down to business. I was so proud of her at that moment, and I really wanted to acknowledge what she'd done, even if nobody else would really understand. So before we served anyone else, I took the microphone and explained with a catch in my voice that my big sister got the first piece of cake because she had waited so quietly, so tolerantly until we were ready to serve. Everyone clapped as Margaret grabbed the plate out of my hand, saying, "Thank you, Eileen!" But before too many hearts were warmed by this scene, she was back, spitting out a bite of lemon poppy seed cake, setting her plate down with a clang, and demanding a piece of chocolate.

OUR BROTHER MICHAEL didn't invite Margaret to his wedding when he got married the following year. But he didn't invite children, either, or dogs or bagpipers, for that matter. Michael's was a lovely, elegant ceremony on the patio of a small Italian restaurant in San Francisco, and it was just what he wanted. He did not want to stand up there, facing his gorgeous bride in front of the intimate crowd and wonder when his big sister might run up and give him a big spanking. So he didn't invite her, and she didn't spank him, and everyone was the happier for it. I doubt that Margaret's life was severely diminished by not attending this wedding. Sometimes we just don't get to go.

Our brother Larry got married the same year as Michael and did invite Margaret to his wedding. But for one thing, Larry got married in our hometown. For another, Larry and Heidi had met volunteering during the Washington State Special Olympics and knew many adults with disabilities. Several of the young athletes were invited to the wedding. A particularly gregarious pair of young men showed up two hours before the ceremony and sat in the back of the somber church on the Gonzaga University campus, the same place where Ann had been married. Every once in a while, as we bustled around getting ready, one of them would call out "Hiiiiiii, Laaaaaarry!" from their pew. Needless to say, Heidi and Larry were both prepared for some dynamic behavior. Margaret was there for photos, but only for a few, and she did just fine. It was the rest of us, bridesmaids and groomsmen, who suffered through two hours of posing in the hot sunshine.

Michael, Ann, and I each had a role in the wedding, so Ann's friend Lori, the same one who had been Ann's bridesmaid, volunteered to sit with Margaret so that my parents could concentrate on their son's sacred union. Margaret was safely ensconced next to her before the rest of us Garvin sibs marched up the aisle. Even so, we couldn't help but watch her as we stood up at the altar of the church, which was as hot in the summer as it had been cold in the winter. During a quiet moment of the ceremony, we all saw Margaret reach out quietly with her right hand and try to pinch Lori under the chin. Lori appeared not to notice and kept looking straight ahead and didn't blink an eye. I flinched in empathy; Margaret had occasionally nailed me before in that same soft spot, and it hurt like hell. Plus, you couldn't see it coming.

Oh, no, I thought, *Here we go.* But then, *wham!* Lori caught Margaret's wrist with her hand, and *wham!* she anticipated the left sneaking in for the finish. She didn't even take her eyes off the altar. Margaret snickered, but not loudly. I tried very hard to look at a spot on the wall at the back of the church so that I wouldn't lose my composure and start snorting. And I could sense Larry, Ann, and Michael doing the same. Our sister kept trying, unsuccessfully, to pinch Lori during the rest of the service. But she did not sing, or laugh, or make any noticeable noise that I remember. Maybe she was having too much fun messing with Lori.

Of all the wedding receptions, I think Margaret had the best time at Larry and Heidi's. I know I did. It was an enormous affair at the Spokane Country Club. I felt like I was at a football game. I passed people I hadn't seen in years, swept along in the buffet line, and shouted, "Hi!

I'll meet you by the bar!" only to be carried along in the current to the dance floor. It was a great party—fun and raucous with lots of people misbehaving and everyone looking gorgeous. One of the Special Olympians lost a beer-drinking contest early in the evening and took off all his clothes in the men's room. Someone had to call his mom to come pick him up, but she was very cheerful about it. Another guest, a young intern from Larry's law firm, got drunk and jumped naked into the fountain later that evening. This didn't go over so well. We Garvins are not as tolerant toward those who should know better, mostly because we have to give so much rope to those who don't.

Looking back on this, I remembered that I'd done all my misbehaving the night before, so I sipped soda water and nursed a hangover, people-watching and enjoying my family. Larry looked so handsome in his tuxedo, and so did Michael, the best man. Our parents were absolutely glamorous in their fancy clothes, although both of them later confessed that their feet were killing them—my dad with his gout, and my mom not used to her sexy high heels. All I saw of Ann was her back as she dragged her jet-lagged and wailing children out to the car. My second cousin's kids held me hostage for a good fifteen minutes telling me a gruesome story about a nest of 'coons in the attic and how their gun-toting dad had taken care of them. But here was my beautiful and hugely pregnant cousin Kathy and her husband, David. My hilarious cousin Pat and his wife, Karen, had brought their lovely little girl, in whose face and name I saw my great-grandmother. There were babies everywhere, aunts and uncles, and my tiny, wonderful grandmother gripping her wineglass by the stem and beaming nearsightedly at everyone. It was a regular wedding reception. *See,* I thought, *we can be normal.*

Margaret had on a lovely plum-colored skirt and a matching jacket. She wore black hose and black flats. One of the staff members at her group home had helped her put on makeup. She was actually smiling, somehow not put off by all the noise and the people. Lori told us later that they had stopped for cupcakes between the church and the country club in an attempt to fend off any cake-related anxiety, and I imagine that the sugar had helped improve her mood.

That night as I watched my older sister Margaret, my heart was full. It made me happy that she could some-times blend in with the rest of us and not have everyone staring at her, making her seem like the odd one out. Although she couldn't express complicated sentiments, I imagined she liked to feel included just like the rest of us did. I felt a surge of gratitude toward my new sister-in-law for making room in her life for Margaret.

Later, when the groomsmen and bridesmaids were making toasts, Margaret hustled in close so she could get right up next to the cake. All eyes were fixed on the lovely couple as their friends and siblings took turns telling funny stories and expressing their good wishes. Cameras flashed as people recorded the special moment.

I'd like to believe that everyone was so intent on the words of love and encouragement pouring into the microphone that probably not very many people noticed Margaret. My dear sister, who had edged in right next to the bride and groom, was waiting tensely, eyes on the cake, with the hem of her skirt tucked down into the front of her pantyhose.

Michael's wife, who was standing next to me, noticed, too. "Oh, no," we said in unison. My mother was standing closest to Margaret, and I tried desperately, silently, to get her attention. Mom saw me gesturing wildly and misunderstood. Thinking I was pointing to the bride and groom, she smiled at me, her eyes shining with joyful tears. "I know," she mouthed. "Just beautiful!"

4.

winging it

In conversation, as in most things, the middle road is best.
Know when to listen to others but also know when it is your
turn to carry on the conversation.

—*On Conversation*, EMILY POST'S ETIQUETTE

S OME OF MY relationships have become trapped in the amber of my memories, and comparing the present with the past can be confusing. My fiery dad, for example, somehow became a mild little white-haired person who makes polite dinner conversation with me instead of insisting everyone shut up so he can watch TV. My ever-tired mother, who ignored my decades of nagging about exercise, is now a road-biking demon with calves of steel. We are all always changing, I know. Even Margaret, who appears to stay more the same than most people I know, is moving through time and space in her own individual life just as I am moving through mine.

I was thinking about this one day as I sat in my back-yard in Oregon, watching the swallows dip and swoop over the garden. Their graceful flight paths reminded me of my childhood and the endless hours of summer sunshine during which I had had no greater responsi-bility than to sit on the dock and watch the birds. Of course, I was supposed to be watching my big sister, too. That much was always understood, if unspoken. Before I was conscious of being conscious, I knew enough to worry about losing track of Margaret. We siblings were all equally terrified when she wandered off on her own. Where did she go, and who was going to get in trouble for it?

My *Birds of Oregon* book told me that the birds I had watched as a child were the subtle-colored cliff swallow and the brighter, blue-feathered tree swallow. Arriving each spring at our lake cabin, we always found a new nest above the front door, created before we finished our own migration for the year, putting the boat in the water and navigating the icy spring waters of Lake Coeur d'Alene, our life jackets bunched up around our small ears. Swal-low eggs incubate for only about two weeks, and the babies stay in the nest for about three more. Compared to our human lives, the entire childhood period of these little creatures is truncated into just a month and a half, which makes me realize I must have been watching many different bird families each summer above the front door, not just one. But at my house it was definitely only one family, the same family.

That's part of what is so difficult about being a child in a big family: Wherever you go, there your siblings are. The ill-informed (probably "only children" themselves) might argue that this is the magical part of being a big family. But I'll bet those people have never had to engage in a physical battle for couch space. As children, my siblings and I were afflicted by the constant and involuntary presence of one another. We crowded together around the same sticky dinner table, fought for position in front of the TV, and struggled for our hard-won minutes in the lukewarm shower while someone else was banging on the bathroom door. We loved each other, but that concept was buried deep during the moments that we battled tooth and nail for the last bottle of Pop Shop pop.

By the time I'd moved to Oregon, those days were long gone, and now we had to go out of our way to get in one another's lives. As adults, my brothers and sisters and I inflicted ourselves on each other by choice. One way we did this was by forcing one another to participate in our hobbies. This was why I was willing to watch *The Lord of the Rings* with my oldest sister Ann's family ad infinitum. And why I let Ann pay for me to get a French manicure for my birthday, even though whenever I looked at my nails I felt like a hooker. It's also the reason why Ann, who now lived a couple of hours away from me, agreed to come to my book club. I had told her—my beautiful, conservative, army-wife sister—that we would be camping, but maybe I just assumed she'd infer the rest—that anyone who would camp out in the woods for book club would necessarily be a bunch of tree-hugging liberals. If she didn't suspect, it didn't show; she was so gracious at the all-organic potluck and our ensuing discussion about the evils of the logging industry. She didn't even bat an eye when, after we'd eaten our s'mores and the kids were tucked in, someone lit up a joint; she just excused herself politely and went to bed.

SINCE I'D MOVED back to the Pacific Northwest, it was easier to connect with my siblings, at least geographically. But getting together with Ann, for example, was much easier than trying to spend time with Margaret. For one thing, Ann would answer the phone when it rang and usually didn't hang up on me. Moreover, with Margaret this kind of interest-sharing business was fairly one-sided. With her autism, she didn't have the kind of empathy that would make her suffer through something she didn't feel like doing just for the sake of another person's happiness (as Ann did by riding in my dog-hair-covered van into the darkening Gifford Pinchot Wilderness with my beloved mutt Dizzy inching deeper into her lap with every mile). That's simply too abstract a concept. But I had non-autistic friends and relatives who were less empathetic than she was, so I wasn't ready to give up on this project, not quite yet. I decided that the next time I went home, I was going to try to get Margaret to go hiking with me.

I had tried it once before, the summer before I moved back to the Northwest and was home visiting. Hiking was something Margaret and I had never discussed, so I didn't know if she knew exactly what I meant when I asked her to go, but she was game to try. At least that's the way it seemed before she slammed down the phone. "You're going hiking with Eileen! OKAY!" SLAM!

As with our then-recent lunch date, I found myself focusing on low expectations. *Just get there first and see what happens,* I told myself on the car ride from northern Oregon to eastern Washington. On the appointed day, I drove five hours to get to her house, knocked on the door, and waited for her to open up. She yanked the door open and peered out at me through the screen. She didn't say anything. There was no "Hi! How are you! How was your trip? Come on in while I grab my things." We don't have those bridges of small talk, no stepping-stones of cheek kissing and shoulder squeezing. She just looked at me for a few long, silent seconds. Then she said, "You're going hiking, Eileen?" When I said yes, she grabbed her purse, brushed past me, and got in the car, slamming the door as hard as she could. Then she didn't speak to me for the rest of the drive, which was really lovely.

Margaret does not talk much. She is definitely not on my top ten list of great conversationalists. If you ask her a question, she is apt to answer yes or no at random. So the questions "Do you want eggs or pancakes?" and "Are you going to stop spitting, or do we have to leave right now?" will elicit the same answer: "Yes?! No?!" So I wasn't surprised or put off by her silence. Which isn't the same thing as saying I didn't wish for more. I hadn't seen my sister for months. Given the choice, I'd like to know what was going on in her life and her heart. What had she been up to since we last saw each other? What was making her happy? Or sad? What had she been doing with her housemates on the weekends? But these are the kinds of questions my sister simply couldn't answer. I had to make do with the limited information I got from the staff members at her house, who saw her every day. I had to hope that she was finding joy in her own way.

ALTHOUGH I WISHED for a foray into my sister's thoughts, part of me didn't mind Margaret's quiet on this particular day. I think we could all use a bit more silence, frankly. The world is a noisy place, becoming ever more cacophonous with our cell phones, laptops, and iPods. My father-in-law can't sleep unless the television set is on. My husband likes to read his e-mail and talk to me over breakfast while he listens to NPR and sends text messages to his chess club members. My nephews play Xbox for hours at a time and watch the same movies over and over again, often wandering away from the TV halfway through the film, leaving the volume up. I'm frequently in the car with friends or family and realize that everyone but me is talking on the phone.

I'm misplaced in the technology generation. I usually drive my car with the radio off. I recently drove thirty-two hundred miles alone without even popping in a CD. I work in a quiet room, the silence broken every now and again by the sound of my dog snorting herself awake or the cat crying to be let out, and then in, and then out again. I leave my phone off when I'm driving, writing, or—wonder of wonders—talking to another live person. Often I'll have several messages when I turn it back on, but none of them urgent, unless you count the ones from Brendan demanding to know why my phone is off.

I grew up in a noisy household, which is part of the reason I crave quiet. But there is something more there, and it's about observing human behavior, the nonspeaking parts of communication. The beauty of the pause, the nonverbal cue, escaped me in my younger years, but I appreciate these elements more and more as I age. I learned from Navajo students at the University of New Mexico how abrupt and foreign an Anglo style of communication could seem. To them, Anglo students and teachers talked too much and too fast. While the Navajos were waiting quietly for what they deemed the appropriate cultural pause so they could respond to a question, the Anglos would get nervous about the quiet and start chattering again, asking more questions. Then the Navajo students would have to wait some more, prompting more nervous chatter and an unfortunate cycle of miscommunication.

When I taught fourth grade in American Samoa my students clued me in a bit about nonverbal communication by teaching me that an eyebrow waggle means "yes." As I'd stand there, hands on my hips, demanding a verbal response, they'd crack up, thinking it was hilarious that I didn't know what they were "saying." I just wasn't listening. I hadn't learned how yet.

My raucous, crowded childhood had given way to a life full of quiet and space and time, three things I'd never thought I'd have so much of. And though I'd been years away from that chaos and close quarters with four siblings, the sense of tension and disruption had stayed with me all along, and I was still trying to shake it.

AFTER ABOUT A half an hour of complete silence in the car, Margaret looked over at me and said, "Hi, Eileen!" Then she went back to looking out the window. I laughed to myself, thinking about how this quiet car ride with my sister was full of irony for me. After all, one of the reasons that my childhood home had been so loud was because of this sister who was now riding along beside me in such a state of tranquility. This scene I was experiencing was one I might have fantasized about, but had never really expected: my quiet big sister.

We drove up U.S. Route 2 to State Route 206 and north out of Spokane as KPBX played Brahms's Piano Concerto No. 2. Margaret looked out the window and watched the scenery as her neighborhood in the quaint college district gave way to strip malls and Chinese restaurants, then big-box shopping centers. Beyond that were the rural outcroppings that had become housing developments, sparsely inhabited, then the last few working family farms, then forest. We entered Mount Spokane State Park and wound up the narrow road toward the ski area. Margaret didn't say a word. Now and then she pressed a finger against the window and whispered something to herself. I've been through a lot with Margaret—violent outbursts, public nudity, explosive vomiting in restaurants—but nothing in our past could have prepared me for this long silence.

During our childhood, Margaret's autism had made her prone to frequent, unpredictable, violent tantrums. They might occur during dinner, in the middle of the night, or in the morning, and often for no discernable reason. Was it her diet? Was it her hormones? Was it her medication? Was it her autism? It was crazy-making to try to predict or resolve the issue that might be upsetting her. But as a child, somehow I felt like I was supposed to figure out what she needed. So did my other siblings. What was the magic trick we needed to do that would make her world right again? We tried everything, and when nothing worked, we tried it all again. What else do you do when someone is screaming bloody murder if not try to figure out how to make her stop? But we were children, not autism experts, and our efforts often seemed futile. Consequently, our collective childhood was marred by the anxiety that plagued my sister and her inability to communicate with the rest of us about what she needed. So now I watched her watching the road, saying nothing, and simply marveled. Deep down, though, I was still as edgy as ever.

I glanced over at her as I drove. Margaret is three years older than I am, which at the time put her at forty. She is taller than I am and heavier, having inherited what our family calls "the McGillicuddy figure." That means she looks like the women on my maternal grandmother's side: tall, large breasted, carrying a little potbelly, and pencil-thin legs. She wears her brunette hair in a short, stylish cut, which highlights her lovely green eyes. Margaret often stands with her hands clasped in front of her, over her large bosom, looking for all the world like the Venus of Willendorf.

In the previous decade or so, we'd gone through extended periods of time without seeing each other, and I had held this image of her in my mind's eye. When I lived in New Mexico, the distance was an obstacle. As a poor graduate student, I had the time to travel but often lacked the funds. Then I got a job with decent pay and a measly two weeks off a year. Margaret could never travel alone, and even with a chaperone, unpredictable plane travel was an adventure that no one was eager to try with her, especially post-9/11. But here I was, living just five hours away, trying to connect with my sister. And with only her. One-on-one, to try to bookmark the past apart from the present, the way things had always been from the way I hoped they might be.

JUST AS I wanted an adult relationship with Ann, Larry, and Mike, I was looking for a change in my siblinghood with Margaret. In the recent past, visiting with my sister had left me feeling stressed, kind of like doing a beer bong and then getting on a roller coaster. It was her outbursts that got me. "Behavioral issues" was the polite term we used when we became adults. In plainer terms that meant a visit with my sister usually included one or all of the following: being spanked, hit on the head, spit on, shoved, ignored completely for the entire week, laughed at, or pinched in that tender area between chin and Adam's apple. (This is probably not something many people worry about, the Neck Pinch. But if you take the time to locate this spot on your neck, you'll notice that it is, in fact, a very tender piece of corporeal real estate. Now imagine that you are just sitting around, minding your own business, and suddenly you feel like that delicate part of your neck is caught in a car door. That's what the Neck Pinch feels like.) All those things might be repeated, at random, for the duration of a given visit. Let's just say it was difficult to relax and have fun under these circumstances, and it was even more difficult to feel warmth toward the perpetrator of such assaults, even though this might be the only time we'd get to see each other all year.

But all these possibilities were preferable to the screaming. When Margaret got really out of control, she screamed this kind of primal scream that made the hair on the back of my neck stand up. Actually it made the hair on my face stand up. And I didn't even know I had hair on my face. This noise also made me sweat in a sudden burst—a sweaty outburst, if there is such a thing. Somewhere deep down inside, I felt I was supposed to do something drastic, like run back into the jungle and drown my baby monkeys because the end of the world was coming.

When Margaret screamed, it sounded like she was trying to turn herself inside out by the force of her voice. And if that didn't work, she was going to keep screaming until she turned the rest of the world inside out. Often when she got like this, she simply couldn't stop. And all I wanted to do was help her stop. But rushing to her aid felt like running back into a burning building to try to turn off the fire alarm and, in my experience, was about as useful. The last time I had tried to help when Margaret was freaking out like this, I had earned myself a twisted ankle and a bruise on the back of my head; Margaret shoved me over backward when I crouched down next to the chair she'd thrown herself into and tried to reason with her.

I didn't know how often Margaret acted like this anymore. When we were younger, the screaming had been a part of everyday life, along with the maniacal barking of the dog, my sister's incessant record-playing, and the whine of my father's power tools in the basement. The combination often made me feel like hiding in a quiet corner, only I couldn't find one in our crowded house. Margaret's tantrums were definitely the worst of all the above, and they were certainly tied to her autism and to the pain or discomfort or anxiety that she simply couldn't explain to the rest of us. Fat lot of help we were, standing around, alternatively soothing, yelling, cajoling, pleading—or, as in my recent case, getting too close for comfort—as she tried to cope with whatever mania was coursing through her at the time.

It wasn't just the screaming that was hard to deal with. In our young past, the waiting was often worse than the outbursts themselves. During every holiday, every birthday, every family outing, the rest of us had this feeling that something bad was about to happen. And we were usually right. We just couldn't say when it would happen. The waiting made us nervous and jumpy. When I finally left for college, I felt like I'd been holding my breath for eighteen years.

After the rest of us left home for school and then working life and marriage, Margaret often became very upset whenever we came home to visit. She would come over from her group home, and we'd all come from our respective towns in states or countries far away. At some point in the visit, something would set her off like Old Faithful at Yellowstone, and the family would act out our choreography of dysfunction and unhappiness. I knew my family was unremarkable in this. Adult children returning home to visit are usually on their worst behavior, drawn back into a role that no longer fits, like an itchy old sweater you can't bring yourself to give away, even though you have nicer stuff to wear, and it doesn't go with anything else in your closet. You check your real life at the door when you cross the threshold of the childhood home. I knew that was how I'd felt. I would feel especially upset to see Margaret continuing to act out. I'd think, *Man, I can't believe she is still doing that.* She was probably sitting across the room from me, thinking, *My God! I can't believe she is still acting like this.* And then she'd get up and rush across the room to give me a big smack on the rear.

Remembering this, I have to admit that although I hate being spanked, watching Margaret spank someone else is absolutely hilarious. Most adults have lost that sixth sense we carry as children—the radar that alerts us to the fact that a sibling/cousin/friend/schoolmate has targeted us, is zeroing in at warp speed. Most grown-ups have forgotten to walk around with their backs to the wall to fend off a surprise attack. In this naïve and thoughtless way, they are usually completely unprepared for what they feel when Margaret swings into action. Her victims are so innocent, so vulnerable, that she has plenty of time for a running start and a complete windup: A grown man standing with a beer in his hand chatting about stocks and 401(k)s with my brother at the barbecue has no adult context for the sensation of being whomped on the rear by a near stranger. He jumps around, spilling his beer, with a child's look of fear on his face. His fear turns to embarrassment, as if he must have done something to deserve this unexpected reprimand. Then it dawns on him that he is thirty-six, not six, and hasn't done anything to deserve that. A look of anger creeps across his face. And there stands my big sister, hooting with laughter. "You don't hit people on the bottom! That's bad manners! Ha! Ha! Ha! Ha!" But what can he do? She's not "normal," right?

This kind of behavior, however, was normal for us. So when I came home to visit and Margaret behaved badly, I'd get angry and sad at the same time, even though she often made me laugh, too. I'd yell at her or not, but I'd feel incredibly pissed off either way. If I yelled at her, she'd usually laugh at me. And if I tried to ignore her, she'd keep doing whatever it was she was doing, trying to get a rise out of me. I just wanted it to end, the misbehaving, so that we could all try to enjoy one another's company. I'd leave feeling shitty, wondering if my presence was bringing out the worst in her. So now I was trying to think of how we could change things.

That was part of this whole interest-sharing concept. This effort at normalcy was a challenge for all of us siblings, because although we functioned well enough in the world separately, when you brought us together we were a bit off. We tended to act like foreign exchange students in our own country: "Oh, I see; it is customary to purchase a card and even a small gift on the anniversary of the birth of a relative or other special acquaintance." Or, "At mealtimes, all persons enjoy eating and drinking and even visiting for an extended period of time around the table. Usually none of the participants throws food at the others." So we tried to act normal, and though we were not fooling one another, it helped to go through the motions. We went out to lunch. We went out for coffee. We shopped. We visited our grandmother. We'd become more collectively normal, at least on the outside.

The first few times I hung out with Margaret away

from my parents' house, she shocked me with her calm. There was no hair pulling at the lunch counter. No spitting of soda back into the glass or weird grabbing motions or funny noises. One afternoon she sat at a restaurant with me, Ann, and Larry, just eating her food and smiling. Every once in a while she'd look up at us and grin. "Hi, Ann! There's Ann!" she'd say, with real joy, over and over again.

NOW, IN THE car, we wound our way up to the top of Mount Spokane, and I decided for myself that her mood was good. I found myself wanting to believe that this new version of my sister—the quiet Margaret, the calm, happy Margaret—was the *real* Margaret. The staff members at her group home had remarked upon her mellowing in the last couple of years. And when we went to the Starbucks near her house recently, I'd been impressed by the sense of being on her turf. The barista said, "Hey, Margaret! How's it going? Grande decaf vanilla latte, right?" And she didn't say it in that "I'm-being-nice-to-the-handicapped-person-because-I-am-kind" voice. She just treated her like a regular, because that's what Margaret was. Margaret answered her, too, and remembered the woman's name. I didn't feel compelled to answer for her or say, "Margaret, tell the nice lady what you want, and stop shredding your napkin," as I might have done in the past. I always feel like such an ass when I do that, like I am betraying her by trying to get her to act "normal" for the sake of other people. But I was the odd one out this time, a stranger who had to spell out my drink order for Margaret's barista pal.

Hiking was taking things to a whole new level. But then I reasoned that it was likely she would refuse to get in the car with me when I got to her house, so the odds were I didn't have much to worry about. She might just say, "Nothankyou, Eileen," and slam the door shut in my face. I was prepared for her to refuse and told myself that was just fine, that I would try again some other time. But she had already exceeded my expectations by coming with me, and I was feeling buoyed by that.

Despite my happiness, my fear stayed with me. After all, it was just the two of us. Though Margaret was once inextricable from my daily life, I was no longer accustomed to spending time alone with her. As we rode in silence, I remembered a time I had taken her with me on a study date during high school, which had seemed like such a good idea at first. We went to the Coyote Café, where I worked, and I even got them to let us sit in a part of the restaurant that was quieter. I thought she would like to listen to the music (classic rock) and eat chips and salsa and color in her coloring books while I studied for my AP exams. We were there for about five minutes before she started laughing—loudly and hysterically—and spitting great foaming mouthfuls of Coke at me and onto my books. She wouldn't stop. Or at least I didn't wait to see if she would. Call me a coward, but I couldn't take it that other diners were staring, that my co-workers were taking turns coming out into the lobby to gawk at Eileen's weird sister. We left.

That was years ago, but I was worried about what might happen and if I would be able to handle it. I was afraid and trying to pretend that I wasn't and simultaneously wondering if I would be able to handle the thing I was pretending not to be worried about. But at least things had started out smoothly today. There we were, two adult sisters out for the day, listening to the radio and enjoying a long drive on a summer's morning. We drove to the summit of Mount Spokane to take in the view.

Mount Spokane is the southernmost peak in the Selkirk Range, which stretches up into British Columbia and Alberta. At its peak it rises to a height of nearly fifty-nine hundred feet and stands high above the nearby collection of small lakes—Newman, Hauser, and Spirit. We had grown up just miles from here, but I had no recollection of coming up to the mountain. Isn't that how it is? You need to be a tourist in your own backyard to figure out where you came from.

Margaret and I strolled a short trail near the summit and drank in the wild palette of silver-leafed yarrow, scarlet Indian paintbrush, and lacy spirea. With my little black dog, Dizzy, in tow, we listened to the wind in the towering Ponderosa pines. In the higher altitude it was sunny but chilly for July, something I always seemed to forget. The wind whipped through our hair as we climbed up to the stone lookout house. It was dark and cold inside. *Empty*, I thought. Margaret loved the echo in the long, low room, and she called out, "Well, hello, there!" to hear the sound of her own voice bounce off the chilly walls. "Hel-LOW, there!" She laughed. I laughed, too, because she sounded so normal and so cheerful, but she wasn't talking to anyone. She was just loving the sound of her voice.

I noticed a father and his two little boys standing in the lookout. I smiled and said hello, but the dad just looked at us with suspicion and didn't say anything. The kids stared; the youngest one said, "Hi." "Hi!" I said back. The dad said, "Let's go, boys," pretending like he didn't see us or hear me. Margaret didn't care; she was saying, again, "Well, HELLO, there!" and laughing. But it bugged me that he ignored us. It always has bugged me, being the "normal" one and watching the adults who decide that the best way to deal with the strangeness in my sister is to pretend she doesn't exist.

The wind and shade of the lookout cast a chill, so I gave Margaret a long-sleeved shirt, which she pulled on and zipped up against the cold. It was too small and stretched tight across her big boobs, but she didn't seem to mind. We headed back to the footpath. Dizzy jogged along in front of us and circled back to check on us when we lagged too far behind. Dizzy sniffed Margaret's hand as she passed, and my sister patted her gently as she danced her little canine foxtrot down the trail. We were silent listening to the wind, the creaking of the branches, and Dizzy's prancing feet in the dust sending up puffs of red-brown dirt. Somehow the scents and colors seemed to intensify, too. We left a quiet in our wake.

For once I didn't feel like I needed to say anything, and Margaret was all contentment, letting one moment lead to another, not having to ask what came next, when we were going home, where the car was, where Mom was, where her staff members were. I had a great time. She had a fine time, too, I think.

Please don't think it was perfect. After all, life isn't a Disney movie. I had to close my eyes and count to ten when Margaret decided that she really did not like the gourmet turkey sandwich I had brought for our picnic and, to demonstrate her displeasure, threw it at my head, mayonnaise side up. Yes, there are undoubtedly more appropriate ways to demonstrate one's culinary preferences, but at least she didn't yell or hit me. Or throw her soda can into the brush so I would have to scramble after it. She just looked at me with a bit of outrage as if to ask why in God's name I would offer her such a piece-of-crap sandwich, and then she threw it at me. I kept counting after the focaccia bounced off my hair and into the bushes, and ultimately decided that $6.95 was a small price to pay for the peace and quiet that Margaret and I had shared up to this moment.

Dizzy was happy to take care of the rejected bun and its contents, and Margaret seemed content with the soda, chips, and cookie in her lunch box. I didn't even say anything about the sandwich throwing. I just wiped the mayonnaise out of my hair with my napkin and handed over my bag of chips when Margaret had finished hers. She grabbed them from me without a word, tore open the bag, and ate them one by one while Dizzy sat and watched for crumbs. We all finished eating in a peaceful silence.

I still found the "peaceful silence" part amusing. This was the person who had kept me from getting a good night's sleep for eighteen years and had sabotaged nearly every family holiday and special occasion with some bit of wild behavior. Now, here she was, sitting across from me at a worn, splintery picnic table with the wind and the sun in her face, offering me this tremendous, unlikely gift: her happiness, her contentment, her quiet. Life is nothing if not surprising.

We drove home, down the mountain, past the farms, into the city limits, where the neon lights that lined Division Street were turning on for the evening. When I took her home, Margaret let me come into her house and say hello to her housemates for about ninety seconds, which was a big concession on her part. I knew my limits and didn't try to stay too long. She had her boundaries, and she was able to be very clear about them in her own way. I chatted with her friends as she stood behind me, nervously twisting her hands, anxious for me to leave, but not knowing how to ask. When I said I guess I'd better go, a huge smile broke out on her face. She gave me the bum's rush out the door, her signature farewell. "Okay! Bye-bye! Thank-you-very-much-for-the-hike-Eileen! See you later! Bye-bye!" She gave me a firm shove over the doorjamb and slammed the door behind me with great gusto, nearly catching me in the ass. I stood on the porch, laughing, thinking that with Margaret there is never any doubt in your mind about whether it is time to go.

As I drove away, I kept the radio off and enjoyed the quiet. I thought about my big sister and how she kept surprising me. And I wondered about what we might do the next time I came to visit. I recalled the end of our hike when, as we walked toward the car, we hit a stretch of slippery gravel. Margaret had reached out and grabbed my shoulder to steady herself. Here is another of life's great ironies—Margaret's fears. This is a woman who thinks nothing about walking out into the lobby of the YWCA totally naked, swimsuit in hand, to ask someone to help her put it on. A person who would probably not think about putting out a fire in the kitchen if she happened to be listening to her favorite record. Someone who has no shame about disrupting a holy mass with some laughter or loud talking. This is a person who, as a child, once rode her bicycle downtown and out onto the highway at dusk. Suffice it to say she isn't afraid of most things that other people are afraid of, but give her a slight incline and a little loose gravel and she is a bundle of nerves.

With her feet sliding mildly, she had grabbed my forearm with both hands and sidestepped her way carefully down the slope. After the worst of it was over, she let go of me with one hand and grabbed my hand with the other. She held on to me all the way back to the car. I didn't mind. It was actually very nice having my big sister hang on to me. The physical contact that we take for granted when we are children or when we are with children is not easily sustained between adults. I liked feeling my sister's slender hand in mine, her long fingers twined around my own in a silent request for moral support. The distance we'd traveled away from each other in the last two decades seemed gone in an instant. The years of anger and frustration and disappointment somehow didn't matter for the moment as we breached all that divided us in a few moments of shared quiet with clasped hands.

We walked along like this, not speaking, and the ground leveled out. With the perceived danger past, Margaret suddenly started to sing, and she swung both our hands to the tempo. I recognized it as her version of a Winnie the Pooh song from our childhood record collection.

"Winga the Pooh. Winga the Pooh. Da da da da da da all something fluff. He's Winga the Pooh. Winga the Pooh. Silly silly silly old bear!" She ended with "We're a cer-eee-al fam-i-ly!"

I stood there watching her beautiful, triumphant smile. She threw her head back, laughing loud and long. Then she dropped my hand, got in the car, and slammed the door as hard as she could.

5.

what autism is

If we have a disabled person in . . . our own family, we make
every effort to learn all that we can about his or her problem
to seek professional advice and to make the family as normal
as possible.

—*On Disability*, EMILY POST'S ETIQUETTE

SUMMER TURNED TO fall. I found myself sitting in the dark on a Wednesday afternoon in Portland's historic Cinema 21, a wonderful old art deco movie house. Footlights cast a warm glow onto the columns along the walls, making me forget about the cold outside, the bite of autumn in the air. I was early, as always. I was sitting exactly in the middle seat of the middle row of the three hundred seats, which is just where I liked to be. And which is another reason I like to go to movies by myself—so that I can sit where I please and in silence. I felt an old seat spring poking against my back, and as my eyes adjusted to the darkness, the heavy drape of curtain over the stage glowed a deep red.

The show was about to start. It was called *Autism—The Musical*. When I bought my ticket from the quirky guy at the ticket booth, I asked if he had seen the show, and he said not yet, but that he was sure I would enjoy it. When he said that, I stared at him like he had delivered some kind of message from the other side. I think I made him nervous. After all, how would he know that I was on a quest?

I wandered into the huge, dark theater and found it completely and perfectly empty. For a moment, I felt like all this was happening just for me. As if when an invisible hand drew back the curtain, I would finally find the answers to all my questions about autism, about my sister, about our family. But that particular show is a musical called *Autism—Our Life*. That wasn't playing at the Cinema 21. It just plays in my head all the time.

As for my quest, I had gone to the theater looking for answers. I'd begun asking questions in my head and on paper. Mostly about Margaret. Since my last couple of trips home to see her, she'd been on my mind. We'd been on my mind, our relationship, I mean, and what exactly I was supposed to do next. It wasn't like my phone was ringing off the hook. Margaret hadn't called me. She doesn't really call anybody. Not to talk, anyway. If she has plans with my parents, like Easter dinner, for example, she'll call compulsively for days before. And when they answer, all she'll say is "You're going to have Easter dinner, please!" and when one of them says yes, she'll hang up on them and call back five minutes later with the same question.

So I couldn't very well expect her to make the next move. The ball was, eternally, in my court. But I didn't know what I even wanted or expected. And I was frustrated by the same sense of helplessness that I'd felt for years. I mean, after all this time, shouldn't I at least understand autism? I had lived and breathed it for the first twenty years of my life. It had haunted me for the last sixteen. I had worked alongside my parents, Margaret's teachers, and student volunteers in helping her learn, helping her cope with our alien world. If I didn't know this, then what did I know?

But I found myself with more questions than answers, so I started reading. At first I was almost embarrassed. I felt like Melville's Ahab cracking a copy of *The Beginner's Guide to Fishing*, but I persevered. I read books by parents, doctors, and therapists. I read the life stories of Temple Grandin, Kamran Nazeer, and Donna Williams, people with autism who were able to write from the other side. As the publication dates on the books became more recent, the parent authors were suddenly closer to me in age than they were to my parents. But their basic story stayed the same. It was a story of lack—a lack of information, a lack of assistance from the medical world, a lack of support from family and friends, a lack of cooperation from the school system. It was my parents' story all over again.

But here and there, I saw a glimmer of what I was looking for: siblings. And my own questions clarified.

What did brothers and sisters do? How did they cope? What were their responsibilities, ultimately? What were mine? Then I saw the advertisement for this film. And even though it was playing an hour away from my house in the middle of a weekday, I knew I had to go.

I sat and watched the documentary, my heart full of emotion. If it were a nice feeling, I'd say my heart swelled. But it was more like a bulging, like it might kill me. It was a terrible feeling. Part empathy, part schaden-freude. The plot revolved around a woman, Elaine, who had decided to put on a musical with local kids—all with autism, including her son. The subtext of the movie, though, was the fierce hope and despair of the parents, the unending conflict that autism brought to their families, their marriages, and, of course, their children. Elaine killed me; her face was so full of hope. Her first husband had left. After many years of raising her son, Neal, alone, she'd met someone and become engaged. Now she and her fiancé together defended Neal from the criticism of the fiancé's family, who thought he was just "a bad boy." We had relatives like that, too, who thought my sister just needed "a good crack on the ass."

At one point in the movie, after all of their defending him, Neal did something rotten to a toddler at a picnic, the kind of thing I'd seen Margaret do. Pretending he was going to be nice, he yanked a little boy over by his arm and made him cry. And then the adults were sucked into this vortex of conflict—the toddler's mom, who was trying to trust Neal's mom; Elaine and her boyfriend, who knew he could act better; the little kid, who didn't understand why he had been set up for a sucker punch. And Neal, who couldn't explain why he had done what he did and cried and cried. It was clear that more than the picnic had been ruined. It was just one more tear in the social fabric, the emotional fibers, and the invisible bonds that held these people together.

Watching their stories, I felt like I was at a family reunion, only everyone was so much better looking than me and my relatives, because the movie was filmed in California.

When the lights went up, I stood up, wiping my eyes with my sleeve. Suddenly I realized I was not alone. There was another woman sitting in the back of the dark theater, also by herself, sniffling into a Kleenex. I felt like I should say something. After all, if she was there watching the film, we must be in this together, right? But words failed me, so I just smiled at her and she smiled back, and I walked out of the dim auditorium into the weak autumn sunlight.

AUTISM IS A neurological disorder people are born with that impairs communication and social interaction. The Autism Society of America (ASA) describes it this way: "Autism is a complex developmental disability that typically appears during the first three years of life and affects an individual's ability to communicate and interact with others."

The ASA estimates that as many as 1.5 million adults

and children have autism today, and that number is sky-rocketing. The Centers for Disease Control and Prevention reported in 2009 that autism affects one in every one hundred children. When Margaret was born, researchers thought it was more like one in every ten thousand births. Autism crosses all racial, ethnic, and socioeconomic lines and is four times more likely to affect boys than girls. Most children, like my sister, are diagnosed around the age of three.

A national advocacy group, Autism Speaks, makes the prognosis very clear on its Web site: "Currently, there are no effective means to prevent autism, no fully effective treatments, and no cure."

Autism is not something people outgrow, although depending on the severity of the disorder, people can learn strategies to deal with their symptoms. The most famous autistic person today is probably Temple Grandin, who still struggles with her disorder but has used her doctorate in animal science to become a professor, an award-winning designer of humane cattle yards, and the author of many books. She has also used her scientist's mind to teach herself appropriate social interaction, which was completely foreign to her.

Other people with autism, however, never learn to speak at all. Many, like my sister, will never be able to live without a vigilant staff to help them, because they simply don't have the life skills they need to complete the basic activities of daily living on their own—grocery shopping, bill paying, cooking, cleaning, and driving.

Although autism is a *spectrum disorder,* meaning it affects people in different ways, people with autism demonstrate a number of common characteristics. The ASA and other organizations identify the following among the well known: insistence on sameness, resistance to change, difficulty expressing needs, and repeating words or phrases in place of normal, responsive language. Other behaviors include laughing, crying, showing distress for reasons not apparent to others, and preferring to be alone. Tantrums are another, as well as lack of eye contact, sustained odd play, spinning, and inappropriate attachment to objects. Margaret did all of the above when we were children and retains some of those behaviors as an adult. She has also shown apparent oversensitivity or undersensitivity to pain and no real fear of danger, which are other characteristics.

While Margaret has severe autism and much of the difficult behavior that came with it, she has always shown a capacity for learning new things and for taking on more normal behavior. She outgrew many of her bizarre childhood compulsions that plagued our daily life, like smelling babies' heads in church on the way back from communion. Or stopping in a crowd to run her finger up the back of a woman's leg if she happened to be wearing pantyhose. Although she is still withdrawn at times, she no longer disregards the presence of other people so completely as she did when we were younger. She tends to greet people when she enters a room, sometimes enthusiastically, sometimes quietly. She makes eye contact and responds, as well as she can, to what people are saying to her, depending on her mood. She avoids interaction if she is stressed and sometimes tries to shut us out with music or rocking or tearing a piece of paper into tiny pieces. These ways of coping, while a bit odd, are certainly more benign than some of the things the rest of us do—drink too much, drink and drive, punch people, eat too much, seek the approval of strangers, or some combination thereof.

I'm not going to make any sweeping statements about what Margaret is or isn't capable of. Generally speaking, it appears to me that she is like everybody else I know, that her sense of the world is not static, and that she can learn and adapt to new situations. But I'm no expert, and I don't know what she's thinking. And I just don't want to pigeonhole her, because people have been doing that to her since we were children.

Nobody knows what causes autism, but the generally accepted notion seems to be that abnormalities in brain structure or function are to blame. One recent study blames a deficiency in "mirror neurons," specialized brain cells that might contribute to empathy and communication in typically developing children and explain a lack thereof in those with autism. So what could cause the abnormalities in brain structure or function or mirror neurons? Genetics, vaccines, food allergies, and environmental toxins are some of the more common theories, but no one knows for sure. Search the Internet, and you'll get a different theory every day. One thing is certain:

As more and more children are diagnosed each year, a growing number of people want answers.

AUTISM. TO ME, this word has always taken a long time to say. It is a ten-syllable word. The letters spiral out of my mouth and into the air. I'm afraid to finish saying it, because once I let go of the word, everybody will know something about me. When I say "autism," I feel the weight of the letters resonate beneath my collarbone as if the word is tattooed on my skin. When I hear the word in the mouths of strangers, the mouths of teachers, the mouths of celebrities, my heart constricts. I feel lonely and familiar at the same time, homesick, like someone is talking about a place I used to live. *Autism. Look, I'm showing my scar. My sister has autism.*

Autism. In my mind I see the word spelled out in red-brown cursive with orange speckles sprinkled across a tan background. Autism smells like bouillon power, like spices, like the lingering aroma of dehydrated vegetables clinging to the empty foil soup packet that Margaret carried around for months one year. She needed to have it clutched in her hand wherever she went, her magic feather for getting through the seemingly insurmountable obstacles of an ordinary day: waking, walking, eating, and being spoken to.

Other talismans followed. For a while it was a red plastic hammer from a childhood carpentry kit. She wandered around the house and yard with that scarlet mallet always at her side. Another time it was the worn scrap of a favorite record cover. She'd hold it in front of her eyes, flipping it back and forth, mesmerizing herself. Later, my sister treasured a worn and tattered hardcover copy of *Heidi* that sat on the arm of the sofa. Avid readers, every one of us, we never read that story, partly because it was imperative, for several years, that the book be in plain view at all hours on the arm of the couch, preferably at a particular angle. I can remember that when I cleaned the living room, I would carefully dust the arm of the couch and then put *Heidi* back—just so. *Heidi* was for spinning.

Margaret spun the book on her knee as she sat on the living room couch, spinning and twirling the book in perfect rhythm for hours as she listened to her music. *Twirl, pat, pat. Twirl, pat, pat. Twirl, pat, pat.* The book was a steering wheel beneath her quick hands as she seemed to mimic our mother driving the car. She didn't have to look down to keep herself on course, steering through a confusing world of other people and noise and language. She didn't seem to hear us as we moved around the house and through our lives while she inhabited her own world and held down that corner of the sofa.

Summers she needed to have the orange corduroy cushion at our lake cabin to spin on her knees and pop into the air with her ankles high overhead, catching it on the tops of her feet, perfectly balanced every time. She'd lie on the floor at the bottom of the stairs, spinning, popping, and kicking for hours if we'd let her as music blared out of the speakers in the next room. She was oblivious to all the people who had to step around her to get to the second floor, where the bathrooms were. She never missed a single catch, and when she wore a hole in the fabric with this routine, she chose another orange cushion from the pile and started over. The cushions were, blessedly, interchangeable in her mind, something that rarely happened in this kind of situation; Margaret usually saw through our efforts at substitution and became inconsolable if a particular item went missing.

I tried the cushion myself once and got nowhere. I couldn't get it to spin, and I certainly couldn't catch it with the same finesse. Margaret was the spin master. However, her expertise at cushion popping seemed less cool when I got old enough to realize no one else was doing it. Our friends would stop and stare, puzzled at the sight of one of the "big kids" lying on the floor and ignoring us. "That's just Margaret," I'd say, wondering what they were looking at. What was the big deal? As if to say, "We eat cereal for breakfast. What in the world are you staring at?"

One summer the autistic talisman was a cast-off wig that Margaret simply couldn't be parted from. What must have once looked like hair when it first landed in the toy cupboard now looked like some kind of small roadkill. My sister wore it all day long in the hot summer sun and put it on again with her nightgown after her bedtime bath. Adding the wig to her cushion routine, she looked even crazier. We have some pictures of that summer, the whole family crowded out on the front steps.

Margaret is looking at the camera out of the corner of her eye, one arm hooked around my mother's neck as she smells my mother's hair, the wig askew. She looks like an extra from the *Muppet Show.*

Another year my sister was obsessed with a blue plastic hairbrush—the only hairbrush in our pathologically thrifty household. She had to know where it was at all times and checked on it several times a day in the bathroom cupboard. This, like every preferred item du jour, always had to be in the same place. If ever it was misplaced, my sister became distraught, then enraged, as if this small piece of plastic were the key to keeping her world righted. And of course things went missing. In a house full of children, nothing stays where it is supposed to.

And Margaret would howl. "Where IS it?! I don't know where it IS! WHERE IS THE BLUE BRUSH! DO YOU WANT THE BLUE BRUSH! AAAAAAAAAAAAAH-HHHHHH!" Her screaming could last for hours, leaving her exhausted and the rest of us staggering around like a cyclone had just passed through the center of the house.

Another season, Margaret's autism zeroed in on the strange black bee crawling up the broad picture windows that looked out onto Lake Coeur d'Alene from our summerhouse. She had never shown the slightest interest in insects before, but now she was spellbound. When it stung her hand, she hardly cried at all. Even after her eyes puffed up from an allergic reaction, she was more interested in the bee than what was happening to her. But when she tried to get a closer look at it and smashed the fuzzy creature with a pair of binoculars, all hell broke loose. Her autism wailed in frustration. "The Bee! Where is the Big Black Bee! I don't know where he IS! NOOOOOOOOO! You want the Big Black BEEEEE! NOOOOOOO!" She struggled with the limp bee body, trying to force it to climb back up the window. When this proved futile, she became hysterical and the small bee body crumbled into pieces. I tried to smash the flaky little pieces back together into some semblance of an insect, but it was the Humpty Dumpty of Big Black Bees. One of my brothers located a large black fly and offered that as a substitute, but Margaret wouldn't buy it. She just kept screaming. Miraculously we found another Big Black Bee—dead, but in one piece—and taped it to the window so she could watch it. She wouldn't go to bed until we'd taped the Big Black Bee to the inside of a plastic cup and put it next to her bed on a chair. "*There* he is! Okay! *That's* better now!" she said, taking deep, calming breaths, still stuttered with sobs. Then the autism slept. After a few days she forgot all about the bee, and her quick, impulsive mind seized upon something else. The plastic cup with the bee taped to it gathered dust for weeks until finally somebody thought we were safe and threw it away.

I KEPT SEARCHING for answers, reading whatever I could find. In my deepening appreciation for this disorder, I recognized that autism could be many things to many people. To the parents of people with autism, it often brings a crisis, a life sentence, a tragedy. Being the parent of a child with autism brings loneliness, anger, despair. The parents suffer the loss of the child they will never have, and often they don't even have time to grieve, because they are too overwhelmed with the child they do have along with all the problems she's got.

Autism also brings parents hope and the motivation to act. Marriages are ruined or strengthened. Careers are destroyed or somehow clarified. Friends and relatives disappear or make significant and treasured contributions to the family. Sometimes, somehow, a disability simply becomes blended into the reality of life along with everything else, good and bad. As Helen Featherstone writes in *A Difference in the Family*, "We were knitting Jody, and our new identities as mother, father, and sisters of a severely handicapped child, into the fabric of an ongoing life."

For people who have autism, the disorder is a burden or a challenge, something to overcome, or perhaps not. A battle against the outer world, a system. Autism is the lack, the missing elements of empathy and intuition that allow people to connect with others. It's a different life colored by the expectations of other people that autism means magical ability or stupidity. Autism is a trap or a safe haven. It's a world of loneliness and isolation and a place of creativity. It's a bull's-eye that makes a person a target for abuse or a yardstick of accomplishment through improvement. Maybe it's a defining feature of a personality or just one characteristic of the many complexities that make up a person. Every life is different.

Thinking about this, I couldn't imagine what my sister would make of her autism. Me, I was just trying to see the person who I thought was in there with it.

WHENEVER I MENTION that I have an autistic sister, people always ask me what Margaret is like. What they really mean, though, is what is her autism like. Is she like Dustin Hoffman in *Rain Man?* Does she have weird mathematical talents? What does she *do?* I have stopped trying to answer those unspoken questions, because the truth wouldn't make sense to the curious. The truth is, I don't really know how to explain autism or my sister. I can repeat the accepted definition of autism. I can rattle off new theories that I hear on the news almost weekly. But none of that seems definitive or concrete to me, and none of it seems to describe my sister, the living, breathing person. I only have my experience to go on. And as I grow older, it becomes more important for me to try to explain it to myself.

Autism has long, graceful fingers, thin tapers always moving, lightly tapping the table, the dashboard, a knee, stacking and restacking themselves, braiding and unbraiding, calming my sister as she acts as her own metronome, keeping time to the march in her head that nobody else can hear. She cuts her nails short, ever shorter, sometimes to the point of drawing blood, because she can't stand the way they feel when they grow past the smooth tips of her fingers. *Clip clip clip.* She uses the same nail clippers to trim the fraying ends of her shoelaces, which only makes them unravel further until she screams in frustration.

Autism is Margaret's lovely hands twisted up in fury, clenched into fists, and pounding the walls, the floor, the windows, in a wordless, roaring rage that takes her away from us to a place she can't see anyone or take comfort from those around her. Hands smashing glass, ripping the door off its hinges, punching a hole in the wall. Scabs and scars on her small wrists from biting, smashing, scratching.

Autism sounds like a pair of graceful, slender feet brushing back and forth against each other under the sheets in the dark, not sleeping. Wide awake in the middle of the night, autism is a peal of laughter inspired by some incommunicable joke. It sounds like a scolding whisper in the darkness as my sister rushes back up the stairs in her long flannel nightgown returning from her compulsive journey to the record cabinet to check for a particular record album cover once, twice, again. It is my sister's voice, perfectly parroting our mother's gentle scolding: "Now, you go to bed!" the same cadence every time. "Now, you go to bed." One-two-three-and-four. "Now, you get in the car!" "Line up for gym!"

Autism tastes like blood in my three-year-old mouth when I bit Margaret's arm to try to make her stop screaming, and then I blamed it on the dog. I'm a liar, a bad liar, and I hate myself. It tastes like the metallic rage in my nose and throat when I caught our neighbor taunting my sister, trying to make her eat dog shit. It's the ice water coursing through my veins when I saw the two mean boys from down the street trying to make her take her clothes off in the front yard. I'm frozen. I'm furious. I'm helpless. I'm enraged.

Autism feels like everyone in church is staring, asking, Why can't you make her stop laughing? What's wrong with her anyway? What's wrong with your family? What's wrong with you?

Autism. It's got more than three syllables. It's got miles in it, years in it. It's a road that cut through my sister's life and, consequently, through mine. It drove over our family and changed everything we might have been. I was just weeks away from being born on the day that all the accumulated clinical testing and observation data was handed down as a verdict. *Autism.* But it was there before I was, so who really knows what my life would have been like without it? It's like living in a river valley one hundred years after the big flood and trying to understand what life would have been like if its trajectory had taken the destructive waters a few miles farther north.

Autism has been with us for four decades now, and I don't know what Margaret is like without it. I haven't been able to imagine what she would be like if she weren't burdened with a disorder that makes it so difficult for her to relate to other people. When I was a child I had a fantasy about her recovery. I'd wake up one day and look over to her side of the room from my matching twin bed. I dreamed she'd be sitting there, waiting for me to open my eyes, and she'd be normal, whatever that means. "Hi, Eileen!" she'd say. "I was just kidding around." And then I'd be normal, too. I loved this fantasy. I tried really hard to believe that this could happen, lying there some Saturday mornings and peeking at her through my eyelashes. But I couldn't ever conjure what things would be like after that moment.

I've never known Margaret without the distinguishing characteristics that come with her autism, but I'm struggling to understand her apart from it. While the disorder is inarguably the single most defining factor of my sister's personality and her life so far, I'd like to be able to separate the two. I want to believe I can understand the difference. It's difficult, because I met them both at the same time.

During our childhood, autism was never mentioned without some connection to my sister, and rarely was Margaret mentioned without reference to her autism. But now, as an adult, I can see her struggle around it, trying to reach the surface of the quagmire that keeps her from communicating clearly, from laughing at the right time, from explaining the complicated feelings behind her tears as she stands, facing me, crying in a mute and terrible sorrow.

Sometimes it seems possible to find a bridge between our worlds and to meet each other in the middle. When the car pulls up at the curb, my sister throws off her seat belt and jumps out of the passenger seat, crying, "Hello, Eileen!" Her face lights up with happiness and recognition. The sun catches her brown hair, turning it red. *Here is my sister,* she is saying to herself. I watch her cross the lawn, a joyful, bouncing rush that might turn into unease in a matter of minutes. But for now her face shines with happiness, the sun touches her brightly striped shirt as she rushes toward me. She's all motion.

Here is my sister, I am saying to myself as I open my arms to embrace her. *This is my sister Margaret. She has a disorder called autism.*

I KEPT READING. I was still looking for the voices of other siblings, preferably older, more experienced ones. I wanted to hear from someone who had been through this before and had the answers to my questions: *How did you deal with all this?* I wanted to know, *And what are you doing now? How do you relate to your sibling? Does she talk to you? Can you go and visit her? How do you try to build your own life knowing that hers will always be limited by her disability? What do you do with your guilt, your anger, your sorrow? What is your responsibility toward this person as an adult? What do you do when your parents die?*

At the beginning of my inquiry, I'd read a parents' guide written by medical experts and therapists. The book offered practical advice on diagnosis, treatment, and educational concerns, even legal advice. Obviously this book had not been written for me. Even so, I found myself getting pissed off when I read the four meager pages devoted to siblings' concerns. Here we were, still an afterthought, and I felt not unlike my parents must have—alone and blazing the trail.

But then I began to notice a new trend in children's books written for siblings of children with autism. *At least this generation is getting that support,* I thought. I joined a Listserv, which gave me hope, but after reading the posts for a while, I realized that most of the other users were teenagers. I became increasingly disturbed by the fact that they were all girls and seemed to be experts on autism. Knowing that boys are four times more likely to have autism, I wondered about how young girls get sucked into the caretaking mode so early in life. They wrote about how hard it was to cope with their siblings and the more standard, depressing realities of being a teenager, but they also spent much of their time offering one another advice on caregiving. They offered tips on how to change their sibling's food or medication or routine. They suggested talking to their sibling's pediatrician to help mitigate possible allergies. Many of them were consciously training for the day that their sibling would move in with them after their parents died. They were little adults already.

The way they wrote, you'd think they didn't have a choice but to become the main support for their siblings after their parents died. Some didn't. Some had no other family to depend on and no financial support. And they had never heard of any alternative. I hadn't, either, until

I'd started this particular search. In *Siblings of Children with Autism,* Drs. Sandra Harris and Beth Glasberg wrote that some siblings become full-time caregivers while others provide ancillary social support. Others cut ties altogether. "Whatever choice an adult sibling makes is a legitimate one," they wrote.

But these Listserv girls were too young yet to make those choices. Some of them had harrowing stories about older, stronger siblings throwing them down the stairs, smashing their toys, tearing out hair, and breaking bones. And they were young, so young. Of course we know the autistic brothers and sisters can't always control their behavior. Yet, I had to wonder how this kind of physical violence was shaping them and had shaped me. What do you do when someone beats you up and your parents say, "He can't help it. Don't be angry."?

I thought about how my parents had the means and the foresight to provide Margaret with a place of her own. I was grateful for that, and, having witnessed Margaret's success in her home life, I was disturbed by the writings of some of these passionate teenagers who said they would never, ever let their brother move into one of those awful group homes, where he'd be so lonely and scared. I thought of where Margaret lived, her cheerful, loud house, her girlish bedroom. I remembered the blank look on her face as she sat rocking on the couch at my parents' house the year after she graduated from school and didn't have anywhere to go. My mother struggled to keep her occupied, to fill her hours, and no one was happy. I thought of how joyful Margaret had been when she had a job she liked, and how she now has the power to make us leave her space when we come over to visit. "G'bye!" she yells cheerfully, slamming the front door on our heels. "Thanks for coming!" she calls out from behind the closed door.

I still think about one of the few older Listserv members who wrote to me. She was in her late twenties and hadn't gone to college, because she felt like she had to take care of her younger brothers, both with autism. Her parents couldn't handle them, she said. She described herself as depressed and having no friends. She had spent all her time taking care of her brothers, so she'd never cultivated any hobbies or friendships. She hadn't had the time for a job, since she was looking after the boys, and so she had no work experience outside the home. While it seemed possible that she could have earned some kind of living from this situation, she said her parents kept the money that the government paid each month for each boy's disability. And at the time of her last posting, her parents had started charging her rent.

This woman was totally paralyzed. What could I say to someone like her? "You need to have your own life if you want to be a healthy caregiver for your brothers," I wrote. "And if you want to take care of them, that is a choice you have to make. You have all kinds of choices." "I can't. I don't," she wrote back. "Nothing changes." She stopped writing. Her story kept me awake at night. It made me think about how I used to believe I was supposed to take care of Margaret when we were older, an idea that made me feel like I couldn't breathe. It was only now becoming clear to me that that scenario would be unlikely, and I was grateful for this, because I knew how unhappy it would make me, and I suspected that Margaret would not like it any better.

So, what, then, were my answers? What was my truth? I was not trapped like that woman was. But I was not untrapped. I had some kind of obligation to my sister, although I wasn't quite sure what it was. Margaret had a home and family and people who cared for her. But it wasn't perfect, either. It didn't make a good newspaper story, like the kind of newspaper feature I seemed to read once a year about how some kid with autism was doing great in school, so great, in fact, that he was in the "regular" classroom and was even making friends with his "normal" peers. And how these normal kids were sensitive, compassionate children whose teachers said they were better kids for having quirky little so-and-so in their classroom.

I couldn't read those stories anymore. They made me angry, because they usually focused on attractive, high-functioning children. Kids with autism who scream for hours and throw themselves down on the floor over and over don't interview well. Neither do the ones who grind their teeth, spit on people, bite themselves, and wet their pants right after you take them to the bathroom, like the kids I worked with when I volunteered in Margaret's classroom during high school. But these are the realities for so many autistic children—daily, difficult realities for them, for their parents, and for their siblings.

Here was another not-so-good story: the forty-year-old autistic woman who kept getting fired for pinching people and screaming at work. Or, on the flip side, a forty-year-old woman who couldn't find a job, because there didn't seem to be any companies that were big-hearted enough to hire someone who needed a lot of support at work so that she wouldn't pinch people who talked too much or go to pieces when the paper shredder crapped out. This was my sister's current hard reality.

In the grand scheme, I knew Margaret had a difficult life. But I also knew she had a good life. She had kind people taking care of her, and she had dedicated parents. She had a home of her own, and she had friends. She was a Special Olympian and a medal winner, too, by God. However, none of this would have been possible without years of effort from my family and her teachers, or without the daily attention and dedication of the staff members at her house. And none of it came without a cost. I knew that the sacrifices my family made—that every family makes—were incalculable.

I read more books about autism, and I wrote. I started to understand how early in my life Margaret's autism had changed me. She and I were two of five kids, and even though the other three were closer to her in age, it was me who turned around to wait for her when the rest of them ran toward the playground. While our siblings sprinted for the swings, Margaret sat on the picnic blanket, staring down at what seemed like nothing, not wanting to go with us, not even seeming to notice that we were there. I stood there on the grass between her and the others, not knowing if I should go forward or back.

Now I had begun to untangle the threads of my own life from what I remembered of our dual one. I wanted to wind them onto a new loom in my attempt to make sense of who I was and how autism had shaped me. I also wanted to see Margaret's life for what it was—separate, complete, whole. Autism was a red hammer, a blue hairbrush. It was rage and tears that somehow left room for joy. It was many things, but one thing was certain—autism was never going away, at least not from our lives.

At the end of that fall, I understood that the story didn't have an ending yet. Autism was still taking my sister and me on a journey. It was those miles and years and mountains that we had traveled—Margaret because she didn't have a choice, and me because I was choosing to try to know her. I began then to understand that I was choosing something in a way I'd never been able to as a child. I knew we both had a long way to go, but nobody gets out of here alive anyway. I didn't know what I thought I had to offer her exactly, as a sibling. I was not the most patient person in the world, and not always as kind as I would like to be. I was no expert on autism or on what Margaret needed to feel more at ease in the world. But I was family.

I remembered a story my grandmother had told me. When I was three years old and too young to remember, I came back to the picnic blanket and took my sister by the hand. "Come on, honey," I said. "Let's go swing. It'll be fun."

That was all I had to go on, and it had to be enough.

6.

the sheep is between the table and the hamburger

It is not essential to have a special gift of cleverness to be someone with whom others are delighted to talk. An ability to express interest in another person and to express your own thoughts and feelings clearly and simply is sufficient for ordinary conversation.

—*On Expression*, EMILY POST'S ETIQUETTE

"WHY DON'T YOU shut up?" I heard my big sister mutter, and then she looked at me out of the corner of her eye. My face was red with embarrassment and shame, but something more complicated, too. Regret, the desire to be understood as a better person, or the desire to have actually been a better person. Margaret was sitting in the big easy chair in my living room, refusing to come to the table and eat with the staff members of her group home who had agreed to stop by my house so that Margaret and I could have a nice family visit. Is that really what I had been hoping for when I made these plans?

"Margaret, don't you want a sandwich?" This question came from Tami, the lead staff person. My big sister just shook her head again and, looking at me again, said quietly, "Why don't you shut up?"

MY SISTER MARGARET has a complicated memory full of hidden drawers and magic locks. Within it lies a strange ability to recall some bizarre minutiae and a failure to grasp many everyday occurrences, a quirk that is funny as often as it is heartbreaking. If I called her up right this minute, for example, she'd probably sit right next to the phone and just let it ring and ring. Maybe she would even get up and walk away from it. She has no social trigger, no urgency within her to respond to the sound of that shrill bell the way the rest of us do. This harbinger of communication simply holds no sway.

On the other hand, she might remind everybody, out of the blue, that our dachshund is dead. "Louie died," she'll say. "Louie's dead." It's true, too, about Louie. In fact, Louie is long dead. He was already ancient by the time I was born, a nippy, grouchy miniature dachshund. Even so, I loved him with a child's passion and mourned him when he died.

Years after his death, Margaret would poke her head in the kitchen door from the living room, where she was listening to her music, and say, "Hi, Mom. Hi. Mom . . . Mom? Louie died, Mom. Louie's dead, Mom." My mother didn't even have to look up from whatever she was doing. She'd reply mechanically, "Yes, Margaret. Louie died." And Margaret's head would disappear back into the living room. My sister wasn't fondly resurrecting his memory or sharing her grief about the loss of our first family pet. She just wanted to hear my mother repeat this phrase back to her. Louie died in the 1970s, and Margaret is still likely to bring up his death at Christmas dinner or Easter, for no apparent reason. "Louie died. Louie's dead, Eileen. Eileen, Louie died," she tells me. And she won't let it drop until she gets someone to respond. "Yes, Margaret. That's right. Louie died." The idea is locked away inside her memory and pops up every once in a while like the alarm clock in the guest room that someone forgot to shut off.

Medical experts call this kind of thing *echolalia*, a behavior that is classified as a compulsion common to people with autism. Writer Kamran Nazeer, who has autism himself, describes it as a desire for local coherence: "a preference for a limited, immediate form of order as protection against complexity or confusion."

That might be true about echolalia, but in our family the repetition of these phrases was often the only kind of conversation we could have with my sister, so we welcomed it. And throughout the years, these verbal tics, the things she remembered, piled up to become a kind of historical catalog for our family. As such I've come to think of Margaret as the archivist of the family history, which is not so much made up of a linear sequence of trips and celebrations, vacations, and holidays like normal families might have. Instead, our collective past is cobbled together out of the things that my sister said and did, then remembered—the bizarre and mundane, the hysterical and the heartbreaking.

So, for example, one Easter when my sister Ann called to invite me to dinner, I paused and then I said, "Eas-TER-mass!" and we both cracked up. We were both remembering a particular spring morning that my mother had been struggling to get Margaret ready for church. "Honey, it's time to go to Easter mass." Our sister was really irritated, pulling on her wrists, stamping her feet, resisting, and yelling, "Eas-TER-mass!" in an angry echo of our mother's kind voice. None of us can say "Easter" anymore without at least thinking of this. Similarly, one recent summer I stood in the grocery store aisle next to my brother as we tried to choose a salad dressing. We both sang out, "WISH-bone!" and snickered at each other. Margaret used to say this, flinging one hand high in the air—happy or irritated, I can't recall— but Larry and his law school housemates kept it alive all these years. So we stood there, two decades later, giggling to ourselves in the store. Now we were the ones being stared at, but we finally didn't care.

Over the years these episodes became the unlikely family glue, sometimes because we were all laughing and at other times because we were all made miserable by whatever Margaret was saying; whatever the case, we were in it together, and it was often the only kind of family togetherness we really had. We were like survivors of the same hurricane, strangers who clung to each other in giddy relief after the storm had passed. Laughter was our way of finding some way through what would have otherwise been a dark and endless labyrinth of small disasters, like "Here Comes Peter Cottontail."

This song was one of the lively secular tunes Margaret learned in her music class at the public school she attended. My Catholic school, which I was led to believe was superior in academics and spirituality, didn't have a special education program. So Margaret climbed onto the public school bus every morning in her "play clothes," and the rest of us marched down the hill in our matching red cardigans and blue corduroy pants. In music class we droned our way through churchy dirges like "Make Me a Channel of Your Peace" or shouted "THE KING OF GLORY" at evening concerts. We stood shoulder to shoulder with the other little soldiers of Christ, dutifully singing the praises of our Lord in the dark, damp cafeteria, which smelled eternally of warm bologna and bananas from our brown bag lunches.

Not Margaret. Her set list was full of happy, God-free tunes. This was public school, after all. So while our Easter season brought songs of the joy of resurrection from the dead, Margaret's class sang about retail:

> *Here comes Peter Cottontail. Hoppin' down the bunny trail.*
> *Hippity hoppity Easter's on its way!*
> *Bringing every girl and boy baskets full of Easter joy.*
> *Things to make your Easter bright and gay!*
> *There are jelly beans for Tommy, colored eggs for sister Sue.*
> *There's an orchid for your Mommy and an Easter bonnet, too!*

The song was entered into Margaret's hard drive, and there it stayed. Margaret loved that song and sang it often, and not necessarily at Easter. She'd pull it out any old time, just as she would put on a Christmas record in July, which always made the summer days seem hotter.

One day, when Margaret, Larry, and his friend John were sitting in our twelve-passenger Chevy van waiting for our mother to come out of a store, "Peter Cottontail" morphed into something completely different. The boys grew hot, then bored, as you do when you're a kid waiting for an adult to finish some eternal and meaningless errand. Margaret became anxious, as she often did when she had to wait. Her anxiety turned to impatience, and she started singing "Here Comes Peter Cottontail" to voice her frustration, clapping her hands to keep time. Her singing turned irritated and then angry.

To pass the time, Larry and John started teasing Margaret, which really pissed her off. She started singing louder and louder and clapping harder and harder. Soon she was banging her hands together and yelling, "Here comes Peter Cottontail!" Then, "Here comes Peter COW-ten-table!" All the time, Larry and John were needling her, asking, "Which Cottontail, Margaret? Which Cottontail?" After they got her all wound up about Peter COW-ten-table, they decided to try to get her to say, "Here come the cops! Hide the pot!" Somehow, by the time my mother got back to the van, these two phrases had merged, so now when the boys asked my sister, "Which Cottontail?" she'd say, "Here come the cops! Hide the pot!"

On the day in question, of course, she was in a bad mood. But as the months and years passed and we kept asking her this question, she would laugh right along with us, and so "Which Cottontail?" became a shared joke. It's impossible that Margaret understood why we thought it was funny, but she seemed to think it was funny to make us laugh. Even our straitlaced mother, who wouldn't recognize marijuana if she found it growing next to her petunias, thought this was hilarious, although she scolded us as she laughed. The last thing she needed was to have my sister pull out this doozy in public.

The question remains: Why would we do such a thing to a person made so vulnerable by her disability? How could we, raised to be good young Catholics, take advantage of our poor, handicapped sister? We weren't trying to be mean; we were just being ourselves. So was Margaret.

About 40 percent of children with autism don't speak at all, so Margaret was luckier than some, even with her limited communication. She didn't say a word until she was about four years old. And then she said only about four words, two of which she made up herself, "quadee" and "ninga-ninga." When she did speak, she exhibited echolalia, repeating what had been said to her. She first learned to talk by echoing things her speech therapist had said. At some point she also picked up the habit of cupping her hand and talking into it. My mother theorizes that this might have helped her hear the sound of her own voice better. Whatever the reason, when she does this, she looks like a covert CIA operative talking into the little microphone wired down her sleeve. She still has this habit; sometimes I'll catch her circling a room and whispering into her hand like she's trying to figure out where the shooter is so she can communicate with head-quarters.

As I mentioned earlier, Margaret has trouble with pro-nouns, too, which is also common for people with autism. For example, if you ask her "Do you want breakfast?" She is apt to nod and say, "You want breakfast." All of this is to say that communication has always been difficult for my big sister and that her teachers, staff members, and fam-ily have tried all kinds of things over the years to help her with the give-and-take of conversation and information.

Educational props sometimes failed, as was the case with a book that was supposed to explain prepositions by illustrating different objects being next to, over, under, and beside each other. My mother didn't like this book, partly because it didn't make any attempt to illustrate objects that might be next to each other in the real world. There was a particularly onerous series about a sheep, a table, and a hamburger that were all the same size and scale. Whoever was working with Margaret would point to the page and ask, "Margaret, where's the sheep?" and she'd respond, robotically, "The sheep is between the table and the hamburger," as she'd been taught. She never said, "It's in the middle." Or "The sheep is next to the hamburger and also next to the table," or "My, that hamburger looks tasty sitting across from the table!" She never demonstrated that she understood the relationships; she just echoed what she'd heard.

This all happened decades ago, and yet, when I recently asked her about the sheep, she said, without missing a beat, "The sheep is between the table and the hamburger," and she gave me a little smile. When we were kids, we asked her this question over and over again, and she'd give the same answer, and we'd all fall apart laughing. My sister laughed right along with us. I really don't know why she thought it was funny, but at least we were laughing together, which was just this side of normal. Whatever the reason, the sheep, the table, and the hamburger have stuck around over the years, a testament to Margaret's memory and to our history together, if nothing else.

As an adult, it horrifies me to think about the things we taught Margaret to parrot, intentionally and unintentionally. "Neal Diamond is a foxy woman" was one of them. "This is the fucking shit" was a favorite of mine that Margaret picked up on her own and would intone at random. "Larry's wearing Crustos!" she'd sing, along with "Larry push a penis!" also inspired by our teenaged bathroom humor. "Well, Mike!" she'll still say, perfectly mimicking my mother's surprise at something our brother did years ago that no one can remember.

These phrases were our common language when we

couldn't share much of anything else. And they linger still. Just the other day, when I was riding my mountain bike way too fast and nearly crashed into a tree, a Margaretism sprang unbidden to my lips from deep inside my own memory: "SOME-in-a-BITCH!" I yelled and laughed out loud in the woods all by myself. And one recent morning as I waited sleepily in front of the toaster with a jar of Adams peanut butter in my hand, I thought to myself, "PEA-nut butter and JE-lly!" in a familiar sing-song voice and snorted so hard that my coffee came out my nose.

Yes, we teased her, but we loved our sister and fiercely defended her from outsiders, like the unkind neighbor kids who heckled my silent sister for riding her bike on the sidewalk as she bashed her front wheel up, over, and down off of each non-bike-friendly curb. Or the kids at school who made "retard" jokes. Then there was that scary neighbor mom who chased Margaret out of her house in a bath towel. My sister had simply let herself in to make a (PEA-nut butter and JE-lly!) sandwich while this woman was soaking in the tub. At the time, I remember wondering what she was doing taking a bath in the middle of the day anyway. And it was just a sandwich!

It occurred to me recently that the rest of us thought these things—like the sheep and Peter COW-ten-table— were funny because we could control them. We knew Margaret wouldn't pull out the pot warning unless we conjured it. She wouldn't unleash this particular phrase in public unless we hit the spring lock in her mind that released it. It was like a magic trick we were all in on. And maybe it was somehow a comfort for all the things she did say in public, the endless things she did let loose on us. This comforting certainty was as significant as it was unusual; our collective childhood was full of the unpredictable from our sister—an infinite number of mortifying episodes in silent churches, crowded malls, and sacred ceremonies. They are seared into my memory because of what I like to call the Oh, No Moment— the instant it became clear that Margaret was about to explode with mirth, anger, or impatience and that all eyes were about to turn to us.

Margaret always seemed to get revved up exactly when we wished she'd just be quiet and blend in. This kind of thing was especially hard when we were teenagers—a time in life that is difficult enough by itself. I grew adept at pretending that whatever was happening wasn't happening to me; I became a kind of silent observer in my own life. Shopping with Margaret during a visit with our Portland cousins was such an occasion. They took us to a brand-new atrium-like shopping mall downtown, the kind with a big escalator in the middle and three open floors rising up in a large, echoey glass arch. As we stepped onto the escalator on the top floor, Margaret leaned out over the rail, looked into that wide-open space teeming with people, and hollered, "Get your hands out of your pants!"

She loved yelling this sentence and yelled it all the time. The first time she had heard it, I'm sure, it was probably a quiet reprimand from my mother, a woman of infinite patience, who worried about Margaret's habit of standing around with her hand down her waistband. She wasn't touching herself or anything. She was just standing there with one hand inside her pants, like little kids will do, like my sixth-grade math teacher did, as a matter of fact. But my mom was always working on the little graces to try to help Margaret blend in more. "Life is going to be hard enough for her," Mom would say.

Somehow, unaccountably, this gentle correction had become translated into a command of Wizard of Oz–like proportions in my sister's head. "Get your HAAAAANDS! Outta your PAAAAANTS!" she boomed, holding on to the last word, loving the echo in the mall. When my brothers and I shushed her, she started cackling and yelled it again: "Get your HAAAAANDS! Outta your PAAAAANTS! Get your HAAAAANDS! Outta your PAAAAANTS!" She kept yelling until she was laughing too hard to get the words out. She doubled over, hanging on to us as the escalator descended, help-less with laughter. "Get your ha! Ha! Ha hahahahaha-haha! Get your hands! Hahahahaha!"

My brothers and I felt like the whole world was watch-ing as the escalator crawled to the ground floor and we held up our big, hooting sister. We kept trying to get her to shut up, which only seemed to get her going again. For some reason, it always made Margaret hysterical with laughter when we got mad at her in situations like this. "Get your hands outta your pants!" and her laughter echoed behind us as we fled the mall, the big glass doors finally swinging shut behind us.

The quiet and holy Catholic church provided another regular venue for Margaret's verbal showboating. My parents seemed to think a weekly dose of the Holy Trinity was imperative for their young brood, especially Margaret, who, unlike the other four of us, didn't have religion class every day at school. When I think of it that way, I can understand why they kept bringing her to church, even though my mother often ended up listening to the end of mass behind closed doors in the foyer with the young mothers, their fussy babies, and Margaret.

More than once my sister ran up on the altar and started a lively rendition of some tune, including "Yes, Jesus Loves Me," before my mother sprinted up and chased her off. Another time, when a visiting priest took a little too long with his homily, Margaret stood up and said, in an exact echo of my mother's scolding voice, "That's enough!" Surprised, he stopped, glanced around at the congregation, and, good sport that he was, said, "Well, I can't argue with that." And he sat down. That time, everybody laughed along with us.

What's also remarkable about these songs and phrases is that Margaret's reproduction of them was exact in tempo and pitch. Every time she said, for example, "EAT your GOD! DAMN! SANDWICH!"—an echo of our exasperated father—she bellowed it grandly, holding each word but the second for two beats. She had a talent for timing, tempo, and pitch that was quite amazing and might have been the envy of some musicians. However, this skill could backfire, because she couldn't tolerate any music that was even slightly off pitch, like at holiday mass when we had visiting musicians. We could almost always count on some pimply-faced college student to straggle off key during his "Silent Night" trumpet solo. While the rest of us smiled woodenly and prayed to Jesus that he wouldn't play every single verse of this endless holiday tune, my sister became apoplectic. At the first bad note, she'd stick her fingers in her ears, squeeze her eyes shut, and shriek to block out the sound. "Reeeeeeeeeeeeeeeee! Reeeeeeeeeeeeeeeeeeee!"

To be fair, that's what the rest of us wanted to do, too. But when someone is doing their best, it isn't polite to tell them they suck. My mother would struggle to silence my sister. Everyone sitting near us would pretend nothing had happened, while those sitting farther away would strain their necks to stare at us. The young trumpet player would suffer through the rest of the mass, knowing that as soon as he picked up his horn, that weird kid in the third row was going to sound off like a tornado siren, and the rest of us would look at the floor, look at the pew in front of us, look anywhere but at each other. Because if we did, we would fall apart with embarrassment and laughter.

IN THE HISTORY of my sister's unholy disruptions, one church outburst took the gold in the Garvin Family Hall of Shame. It happened one Sunday during the sign of peace when we all had our guards down. This is the time during Catholic mass before communion when you turn to the people around you, extend your hand, and say, "Peace be with you." As a kid I loved this part, because we'd been sitting in the dark for almost an hour, and it was a relief to be able to move around, stretch, talk to other people, and even yawn openly without anyone noticing. I have to wonder if the Vatican II folks stuck it in there to make sure people woke up before the end of mass.

My mother was always at Margaret's side to facilitate this process, to remind her to hold out her hand, to tell her what to say. But on this particular day my mother must have had her back turned for a nanosecond as she greeted someone. Margaret was sitting near this nice little blue-haired lady, who was, thankfully, hard of hearing. When the woman put out her soft little boneless hand and said, "Peace be with you, dear," my big sister reached out, grasped her hand, and pumped it up and down as she exclaimed, "I'm gonna KICK the SH—!" and would have finished "—IT outta ya!" had my mother not spun around and clapped a hand over her mouth.

We were so mortified by this outburst that we were, luckily, looking at the floor for the rest of mass and could not see our friends and their parents sitting a couple of pews in front of us, the whole family a quaking mass of shaking shoulders and muffled snorting as they tried to contain their laughter. We'd have been done for. None of them ever forgot this episode, and I'm sure no one

who was within earshot ever forgot it, either. Margaret appeared to think about it from time to time, too.
While she was still living at home, she'd poke her head
in the kitchen door with the non sequitur "You be quiet
in church, Mom. That's GOOD behaving." Then she
would wait for our mother's affirmation. "Yes, Margaret,
that's good behaving." And my sister's head would disappear back into the living room.

MARGARET'S TALENT FOR voice and memory was alter-
nately hilarious and mortifying when we were younger.
But by the time I moved to Oregon, I realized how much
things had changed. What was once a source of daily
embarrassment and stress for me had softened into a
fond recollection. My quiet adult life was empty of the
shock and rush of Margaret's actions. I moved through
stores, crowds, and holiday dinners just like anyone else.
Nobody stared at me or the people I was with. No one
in my cohort was apt to throw herself on the ground
kicking and screaming under the clothes racks in Nord-
strom's. Nobody said "Hi, Eileen," in the middle of the
night, as casually as if I were sitting next to her on a park
bench at noon instead of trying, desperately, to get some
sleep. Nobody bounded naked through the living room
when I had friends over, laughing or crying about her
brown bra. I could sit at the dinner table for hours if I
wanted to, and nobody threw food at me or spit on me
or took my plate away before I'd had a chance to finish,
insisting that it was time to go.

But I also found that none of my friends picked me up by the neck in a bear hug, either. Nobody tackled me on the family room floor and rolled around with me, hooting with laughter, telling me, "I'M not your meLON!" When I was home alone, nobody was spinning records to create the soundtrack of my day—Ella Fitzgerald, Simon and Garfunkel, Electric Light Orchestra, Arthur Fiedler's Pops. Nobody continued to apologize over and over again for the last time they had pinched me by giving me the kindest of hugs, the sweetest pressing of a cheek on mine before reaching out to pinch me again.

I found that I missed the craziness and color that Margaret brought into my life. As in any life, the good and the bad of the past were long gone, and I had only the memories of that time. And though the past echoed back at me on occasion, it wasn't always what I wanted to hear.

THE DAY MARGARET refused to eat lunch with me was my second summer in Oregon, back in the Pacific Northwest. I'd been in more regular contact with her through the staff at her group home, trying to find ways to connect with her. So when I found out that she would be traveling to the coast for a week's vacation with one of her housemates and a couple of staff members, driving right through my town, I asked Tami if she would be willing to bring Margaret by. She agreed, and they planned to stop for lunch on their way to the coast.

On the appointed day, I waited, nervous and excited,

as the lunch hour came and went. Hours later Tami called to explain that they had missed the turn from I-90 to U.S. 395 and ended up going a different, longer way. We arranged for them to come by on their way home instead.

A week passed and again I waited by the front door for my sister to appear, half certain they wouldn't make it this time, either. But suddenly there they were. Margaret was all smiles and enthusiasm when they first arrived. "Hi, Eileen!" she said, opening the car door and sticking a foot out on the pavement before the car had reached a complete stop. She threw off her seat belt, jumped out of the car, and gave me a big hug and a huge smile before she pushed past me and hurried into the house.

While her housemate and two staff members were still climbing out of the car, stretching, and introducing themselves, Margaret did a speedy self-tour of my house. We followed behind slowly, moving up the sidewalk and into the house, me asking about their drive, asking if they were hungry, them telling me about their three-hour detour on the way to the coast. By the time we'd entered the house, Margaret had retreated to the living room and plunked herself down in a big rocking chair, withdrawing from the rest of us.

I had set the table before they'd come, but thought better of it right before they arrived and put everything back in the kitchen for a casual buffet. Too much structure made Margaret nervous. The two staff members— Tami and Teri—made sandwiches for themselves and

Margaret's quiet housemate, Ken, but Margaret refused to come to the table. She just kept looking down and shaking her head when they asked if she was hungry. "No!" she said. I knew enough to let her be. I knew what would happen if I tried to get her out of that chair. At least I thought I did. I thought she'd just get upset and start yelling. She might even head for the car and insist on leaving.

Tami and Teri seemed puzzled. "She was so excited to come here this morning," said Tami. She told me that Margaret had gotten up, showered, and was ready to go before the sun rose. But I knew better. Margaret was probably not excited to see me as much as she was just anxious to get on with "the plan." My house was the last stop before home. She probably wanted to get the trip done with in the order it was planned, that's all. And that's pretty much the way our entire anxious family behaved on the last day of a vacation. We seemed to forget how much fun we'd had and would think, "Well, crap! Vacation's almost over! We might was well just go home, goddammit!"

But I didn't say anything. I just watched Margaret and listened to Tami and Teri talk about their week at the beach. They told me things my sister never could: dates, times, names, events. They'd rented rooms right by the water in Lincoln City, Oregon, a place we used to go on spring break with our parents. The four of them had spent the week walking along the coast, watching people fly kites, wading in the cold Pacific, and generally lounging.

"Margaret really liked going for walks," Tami said.

"She liked the wind," said Teri. "She'd say, 'It's blowing!' You know how she says that?"

I did. I could see her standing on the beach, smiling into the wind and pointing a long, graceful finger at the sky. That made me smile. I glanced back at Margaret, but she averted her eyes when she saw me looking.

Margaret's housemate, Ken, who also has autism, always looks really nervous when I see him. He looked a little scared sitting there at my table. I had never heard him speak, but he has a very kind face. Even today, whenever I say, "Hi, Ken! How are you?" he just looks at me with wide eyes and grimaces, trying to smile. Ken had eaten part of his sandwich and was gulping his root beer. Tami said, "Ken! What did we say about drinking slowly?" She gave him a patient lecture about how he needed to drink slowly or he would make himself sick, remember? Ken, looking very sorry, nodded vigorously, crushed his root beer can in one hand, and belched.

During this conversation, Margaret got up and hurried into the bathroom like she was late for some really important meeting. She came out while still zipping up her pants, which earned her a gentle reprimand from Tami about why it's important to pull up your pants before you come out of the bathroom. Then she reminded Margaret to go back and wash her hands, which Margaret did with great urgency.

I guessed that Tami had said these things to the two of them over and over and over again. When I had lived with Margaret, I had done the same: *Cover your mouth when you cough, Margaret. Say, "Please pass the bread," Margaret. Close your mouth when you chew your food, Margs. Wait your turn. Say, "Excuse me." Put your clothes on before you open the bathroom door. Don't push people.* It was like having a kid around all the time, a kid who would never learn, and it was endlessly frustrating for me to repeat the same things without any apparent change in her behavior.

I watched Tami and thought about how I had always imagined this was something I would end up doing—taking care of my sister. When I was in my twenties and people asked me when Brendan and I would have kids, in my head I was thinking that I needed to keep myself freed up for the time that I would be taking care of Margaret. Even years after Margaret was in a residential setting with professional staff, in the back of my mind I felt like I was supposed to be preparing myself to be her caregiver. Why I thought this, I can't say. It's a terrible idea for many reasons, including my personality. Luckily, I'd never been asked to be this person for Margaret. Some parents simply assume that their other kids will step up to the plate and take on this task when the time comes—failing to acknowledge it as an enormous, life-changing burden.

Our parents had had the foresight and the means to make long-term arrangements for Margaret. They worked very hard to provide her with a stable, sustainable living situation, including a twenty-four-hour staff. Even so, my survivor's guilt still pricked me every now and again with thoughts of what I should be doing for my sister because my life is so much easier than hers. But as I watched Tami, I was simply grateful that Margaret had such patient and vigilant staff members who were willing to keep offering the same careful advice to her and to give her some freedom by being there to support her.

We sat at my dining room table, eating our sandwiches and making small talk while Margaret rocked in the chair a few yards away. Then there was a break in our conversation, and I heard my sister say, "Margaret, why don't you shut up?" She muttered it to herself, looking at the floor. And even though she said it quietly, I heard her perfectly, because it was a true-to-life imitation of my own teenage voice. Although I don't remember saying this to her, I'm sure I must have said it—and worse—when we were growing up. "Shut the fuck up" comes to mind. And even "Jesus fucking Christ, Margaret, would you fucking shut the fuck up!" in a more eloquent and frustrated mood. Perhaps I said this when she had been screaming for hours and banging her hands against the walls, the doors, the floors. Maybe I said it when she was laughing and goofing off at the dinner table so I couldn't get a word in edgewise in our already loud family. I can't remember, but she clearly does.

Margaret looked at me out of the corner of her eye

and said it again, just as clearly. "Why don't you shut up?" I glanced at Tami and Teri, who were looking at my sister, but didn't say anything. I wondered if she said this all the time or if it had just popped into her mouth because she was with me. I didn't know why Margaret said it. I didn't know if she was irritated with me because I was crashing her vacation or if she was just anxious. Maybe this was just a meaningless phrase that she attributed to me. Maybe she really just wanted me to shut up. Whatever the case, it made me feel like an asshole to hear this sound bite that I'd left in her head after all this time. It was an inversion of the familiar feeling—embarrassment at Margaret's public outburst—because this time I had no one to blame but myself.

While the rest of us finished eating, Margaret rocked in the chair and shredded a piece of junk mail. I asked her if she wanted to see my garden, thinking she might want to be in a quieter place. "Yes!" she said and jumped up out of her chair. But as soon as we went outside to look at the garden, she got nervous and wanted to leave. She hurried back into the house and said, very politely, "Do you want to go now, please, Tami." It wasn't a question. There was nothing more to be done after that, really. Tami, Teri, and Ken had eaten, and Margaret had made it clear that she wanted to get moving. There was no reason to stay. This, after all, was a family visit.

My sister brightened immediately when Tami said it was time to go. She jumped up and started bidding me farewell before the others had even left the table. Margaret gave me a big, one-armed hug, pressing her cheek against mine. "G'bye, Eileen! Thanks for the visit! Thanks for the lunch, Eileen!" she said. I knew she must be hungry, since she hadn't eaten lunch, and I also knew she would probably get a stomachache if she didn't eat. So I offered her a granola bar for the ride and found myself grateful that she accepted it.

"Okay, Eileen! G'bye, Eileen! Thank you! Nice seeing you!" Margaret kept saying this and waving to me as we walked together toward the car. I hugged her again and said good-bye to the rest of them after giving Tami directions to the highway. "G'bye, Eileen!" Margaret was still saying as they pulled away from the curb. "Thank you very much for coming!" she yelled out the window. She looked so joyful, never so happy as when she was allowed to leave. But isn't that how it is sometimes with family? The best part of the visit, when you feel both affection and relief, is when you get to drive away.

A few days after this visit, I got a card in the mail, clearly dictated by a staff member, because Margaret doesn't usually write in complete sentences. In Margaret's large, signature printing, the following message crawled across two pages: "Here is a pichter of you and me. I really liked visiting with you. I liked your house. Love Margaret Garvin." And then another, "MARGARET

GARVIN!!!" with stars around it. Along with this card was a photo that Tami had taken. Margaret is doing her fakey, I'm-in-front-of-the-camera smile, and I'm leaning over her looking worried.

I taped the picture to the refrigerator and put the card away in a box of letters, grateful that the kind staff had helped Margaret write to me and trying to bury my concern about their spelling skills. I started to write back, and then I thought, *What's the point?* I wondered what it meant to her to get a piece of mail from me. Did she know where I was? Did she understand the concept of keeping in touch? These questions depressed me for days, even as I tried to be happy that we'd seen each other instead of dwelling on my mortification at being the Shut Up Sister.

IN THE WEEKS that passed, I found myself reading more about autism, continuing my quest for information about siblings of autistic adults. One book had a short section on relationships between siblings. In it, a parent commented, "When we explained to our daughter that autistic kids often have trouble responding to other people, I think it was a relief to her. Sometimes I wonder if she didn't blame herself for their lack of a relationship." Reading that sentence reminded me that there is a third party involved here, and its name is autism. So I put some of my guilt in the storage locker where I keep my self-pity and decided to just keep trying with Margaret and see what happened.

A few days later the unexpected happened. I got a voice mail message from my big sister. That was a first. I heard heavy breathing into the phone. Then I heard her high little monotone voice saying, "Hello . . . Hello . . . Yes." And in the background I heard a young woman's voice saying, "Tell your sister hello. Say, 'Hi, Eileen!'" Margaret dutifully said, "Hi, Eileen!" and hung up.

I called back and talked to the young woman, Alicia, who was a new staff member at Margaret's house. "She kept calling me Eileen, because our names kind of sound the same, and so I thought she might be missing you. I asked her if she wanted to call you and she said yes," Alicia told me. Did Margaret really want to speak to me? If this was a gift horse, I wasn't looking for bad teeth. We chatted for a few minutes, and Alicia filled me in on what Margaret had been doing. At the end of our conversation, she asked me if I wanted to talk to my sister. I hesitated. Margaret and I did not talk on the phone. My family didn't have the best phone skills to begin with, but Margaret really hated the phone. I was pretty sure she would get agitated and hang up on me in about five seconds. But I thought, *What the hell. I'm used to being hung up on.* "Sure," I said, and Alicia passed the phone to Margaret.

We said hello, and I asked her what she had been doing, knowing she'd had a computer class that morning. She paused. "You went hiking," she said firmly. It took me a second to realize that she was talking about our hiking excursion to Mount Spokane.

"Yeah!" I said, pleased that she'd remembered. "We did go hiking last summer. But what did you do today? Did you have computer class?"

"Yes."

"Was it fun?"

"Yes."

"Who else was there?"

Silence.

"Who was in your class, Margs?"

"You had computer class."

"Do you want to go hiking again soon?"

Silence.

"Maybe you can come see me at my house again."

Silence.

"I'm really glad you came to see me with Tami and Teri and Ken."

Silence.

"Margs, do you remember coming to my house? Do you know where I live?"

"Yes."

This was a pretty typical conversation. *Yes* and *no* are standard answers for my sister. If you asked her if she wanted pancakes or eggs for breakfast, she'd probably say yes, but she'd really want cereal. I didn't have any idea what she really thought most of the time. This was part of the challenge of having a relationship with an adult with severe autism. Lately it had seemed that she always wanted to go with me when I showed up, but sometimes I really couldn't tell if she was glad to be with me or not, if I should even bother, or if I should just leave her alone. Our last encounter had made me even less sure, but I wanted to keep trying, so on the phone I asked her again.

"Margaret, where do I live?"

She hesitated and then I heard her say, "The river."

"Yeah, Hood River! That's right. I live in Hood River!"

"Hood River, Eileen," she said. "That's the HOOD River."

I was ridiculously pleased that she kind of remembered the name of my town. You'd think I'd won a trip for two to Maui, the way I was beaming. While I was savoring this sisterly moment, Margaret said, "Okay! G'bye!" and hung up on me. I laughed and said good-bye to the air, said good-bye to nobody, and hung up the phone.

As I stood there by myself in my quiet house, a little bit of peace leaked into the crack in my heart. For a moment I felt as joyful as Tommy and sister Sue on Easter morning with their baskets full of Easter joy. Whatever her limitations, my sister did remember me. She remembered the sister from the recent past, the one I was trying to be. That gave me hope and the courage to keep trying to be part of Margaret's life.

Things certainly hadn't turned out the way I thought they would. But some things were much better than I could have ever imagined. We never quite know what lies up ahead. All we have are these minutes and hours we are living right now, and we have to construct our happiness and our cures out of what we've got in our own pockets. Margaret had helped me to see things differently and to understand distinctly how we each need to make our own way. When I thought about my sister and our ever-changing lives, I thought about that old saying about the lemons. I thought to myself, *If life gives you sheep, sometimes you just need to make hamburger.*

7.

friends and neighbors

The Golden Rule is the guiding one when it comes
to thoughtful, cooperative living.

—*On Neighborliness*, EMILY POST'S ETIQUETTE

M Y NEW HOUSE in Oregon was just a block from an elementary school that was across the street from a preschool. A few blocks beyond that stood the middle school. From my desk every day I watched a parade of children and teenagers and parents streaming past my house in the morning and again in the afternoon. At lunchtime I could hear the buzz of the playground and the shrieking of little girls testing their power with their voices. If I walked by at recess I could see them having screaming contests with no apparent goal other than to try to be the loudest one. They leaned forward, squinched their eyes shut, and let fly so hard I expected their braids to fall off.

I found it unnerving, this screaming. It made me anxious. I felt the same way whenever I heard a baby cry, because of my own experience with Margaret's screaming, which often went on all day. The baby might cry itself blue, and the little girls might shriek until nightfall, and I would feel compelled to act. Luckily, I realized that doing anything would have been inappropriate, so I just kept my eyes on the pavement and avoided the playground during lunchtime. The first summer in the new house came as a relief to me, because the children were out of school and it was quiet again. I know this might not seem rational, but for me, at least, it was historical.

Once when I was ten my sister had screamed bloody murder for an entire day about a blue plastic hairbrush. I do mean *all* day. Hours. So loud and long that someone had called the police. There was a lot of screaming at our house back then, but we lived in the kind of neighborhood where people stayed out of one another's business. Because of that culture of "don't get involved," I know my sister's screaming must have topped the charts for someone to actually pick up the phone and complain.

It was a warm Saturday afternoon when the police car pulled up in front of our green suburban house with its tidy lawn, white lamppost, and curving walkway. The large picture windows on the first floor looked out on the whole neighborhood peering in at our wild household.

The screened-in windows on the second floor were wide open, so it was easy to imagine why someone had called the cops in the first place. You could often hear Margaret screaming for about four square blocks. I knew this because once when she was having a fit, I had walked away from the house to see how far I had to go before I couldn't hear her anymore. It was a long walk.

One of the cops climbed out of the car and marched up the walkway to the front door, the one nobody used. He rang the bell and, convinced that someone was being flayed alive on the second floor, insisted on coming in. So we all trooped into the bedroom I shared with my thirteen-year-old sister.

"Margaret," my mother said in her Very Nice Mom Voice—which she somehow almost always managed to use no matter how long Margaret had been screaming or laughing or doing something else that we all really, really wanted her to stop doing—"you were yelling so loud that the policeman came to see if you were okay." Margaret didn't even look at her, or the police office, for that matter. Her mind was elsewhere, thinking about the hairbrush and the crisis its loss had caused. The cop crossed the room and squatted down next to the bed so that he was on the same level as Margaret. You could tell he was a nice guy. He was young, earnest, and handsome. He wanted to know if my sister was all right. Everything was going to be just fine, he wanted her to know. Could she tell him what had happened? My sister turned her head to look at him and took a deep breath.

• • •

THE DAY THE cops came to our house happened to be the same day that my friend Michaela's parents decided not to move back to California. I'm not saying these two events were related, but back then this kind of coincidence took on magical significance for me and helped explain away the unending small and terrible crises that autism wreaked on my family. Decades later, I was surprised that I remembered this particular day at all but saw that I was arrested by the power of small kindnesses of friends and neighbors. I saw how they made indelible marks on our lives.

Childhood can seem interminable. When I was ten it seemed impossible that anything in our neighborhood would ever change. The houses of the people around us formed the edges of our universe and delineated how people viewed our family. The redbrick ranch next door was a rental property, usually occupied by people who were friendly but kept a polite distance and never stayed long. Two doors down lived our surrogate grandparents, people who always had time for us and opened the door before we even had a chance to knock; we knew we were loved by the Henrys.

The Waldrons, across the street, were older and less interested in playing with us, but always kind. The Reimans gave us stale suckers when we came over to watch game shows; their elegant, shabby house was slowly falling apart and smelled of mothballs. Another neighbor always smiled and waved, but she gossiped about us and told people that my parents were getting a divorce because of my sister. The end of one block had a Boo Radley house that scared the beejezus out of me. Huge, overgrown bushes hid the dark front porch. I could always hear the big dogs they kept in the backyard barking as I walked by. But like the house in Harper Lee's book, it was really just a sad house. In it lived a pretty mom who worked too hard and didn't have a husband to help her with her two wild boys. I only saw her walking to and from her car on her way to work. She never spoke to us and seemed not to notice if we waved.

There were many other people in between in this quiet middle-class neighborhood—genuine friends of my parents who cared about me and my brothers and sisters and managed to accept Margaret on some level, despite her differences. The Youngs and the Harms, my parents' sailing friends, knew her and watched out for her, just like they watched out for the rest of us.

Margaret formed her own special relationships with people, too. The Waldrons supplied bananas to my silent sister, who would pop across the street every now and again. The Henrys treated her like the rest of us, welcoming her into the house and spoiling her with soda and candy. So what if she gobbled hers up and forgot to say thank you? They understood.

Years later we found out that she had often dropped in on the Bateses, a family down the block. Their kids were teenagers when we were in grade school and intimidated the rest of us, but Margaret watched TV with them and made herself peanut butter sandwiches in their kitchen.

An older couple down the bay at our lake house later told us that Margaret would come by and make cookies with them when she was an adolescent. Those were the times when she disappeared for what seemed like forever and scared everybody. No wonder she couldn't hear us calling. She was busy mixing cookie dough.

As a child, Margaret did not talk much and could not explain herself. So I imagine these secret friends of hers had been surprised the first time she walked in without knocking and helped herself to a snack. But for some reason they were all able to transcend the gaps of regular communication and connect on some level. She formed this social network on her own, without any of us knowing. Did she consider these people her friends, or was it more simple: the house with soda, the people with the bananas, the teenagers with the peanut butter, Deanna McRae with the Percy Faith record?

The McRae household next door had a big and long-lasting impact on my sister, and on me, too. Smaller and tidier than our big, crazy place, the McRae house was my extended living room for more than a decade. Vanessa McRae, my age, instantly became my favorite person in the universe one summer day in 1978 when she moved in next door. And I loved being around her family, too. Their household of four was so calm compared to ours, and that order came from the lady of the house—Deanna McRae. At five foot two and one hundred pounds, she scared the pants off me when I first met her.

When Deanna got mad at her kids, everybody in the neighborhood knew it. I can still hear the sound of her voice the day she told Vanessa and her brother, Jason, that they had to be in by five o'clock for dinner. "Vanes-SA! Ja-SON! FIVE o'clock! Do you hear me!?" I can hear it now as if I'm still perched in the maple tree I had hidden in. She was so mad at her kids that day that I just assumed I was gonna get it, too. But she also loved to laugh, and when she did she was all sunshine. Moreover, as an adult I understand now that she wasn't exactly angry; she was just setting boundaries and making rules that she expected people to follow. Period. In my house, nobody had time to ride herd on us, and with Margaret's autism and my Dad's short fuse, rules were often a moving target.

Deanna McRae, in her typical fashion, approached Margaret as she would anyone else. She set rules and stuck to them, like when it came to her record collection. Unchecked, Margaret would sprint across the driveway between our houses and crash through the side door. Then she'd rush into the living room, throw open the cabinet, and madly thumb through the family music collection until she found what she was looking for. "There's Percy Faith!" she'd exclaim. "Okay! That's better!" And then she'd slam the cabinet door shut and speed-walk out of the house, not speaking to anyone and slamming the door behind her.

This just wasn't okay with Deanna. So she simply explained to Margaret that she needed to knock on the door, be welcomed into the house, ask permission to search the collection, walk into the living room slowly, and carefully look through the records. She actually walked Margaret through it one step at a time, praising her as she went along. After laying out these rules, she usually let my sister in, as far as I can remember. This was the first time in my life I'd seen anyone get Margaret to consistently slow down. Deanna was like a snake charmer. Of course, Margaret couldn't really slow herself down all the way, and what resulted was a comical mix of fast-forward and pause. She'd sprint across the driveway and come to a screaming halt in front of the door. Then the knock, and when she was told she could come in, she'd throw open the door and fire her request at whomever happened to be sitting there.

Even if it wasn't Deanna, she'd say, "Doyouwant-tochecktherecordsplease, Mrs. McRae!" With permission granted, she would walk as fast as she could walk without actually breaking into a run into the living room to take care of business. Often she would bang the door shut behind her as she left and, remembering, would crack the door, poke her head back in, and say, "You don't slam the door!" by way of apology before she slammed it again.

Occasionally, of course, my sister forgot and rushed

into the house, but Deanna just made her go back out-side and start over. And she did. It was like magic.

Deanna was tough, but I always knew where I stood with her, and so did Margaret. By the time we were in middle school, most of our parents' friends were used to Margaret, but I had the sense that many of them didn't really know what they were supposed to do with her if she misbehaved around them. It wasn't their fault. We didn't know what to do, either. We just tried everything, and nothing seemed to work, so we tried something else. Deanna had somehow found something that worked.

As for me, Deanna never told me to stop coming over every day, although she would tell me when it was time to go home. She never told me to stop decimating the candy jar, which sat on the counter, always full of Her-shey's Kisses and Rolos, and made me edgy with its con-stancy. At my house it would have disappeared forever in five minutes. She just told me to stop leaving my balled-up wrappers in the jar.

There were other things Deanna never said to me. She never congratulated me for being such a good sister, which many adults did when I was growing up. I think they must have felt so uncomfortable about Margaret's weirdness that they needed to make a hero out of me. "You're a very good sister!" they would say with tight smiles. I never knew what to say to that. Deanna also never commented on the chaos at my house, which the entire McRae family was privy to given the proximity of our homes. She never mentioned the screaming or slamming of doors. She never said anything about what she couldn't have failed to notice—that we other Garvin kids were getting the short end of the stick because Margaret's autism took up so much of my parents' time and energy.

My childhood did eventually end, although some nights when I drifted off to sleep, I still thought of that perfect hiding place for kick the can that I discovered down by the Youngs' trailered sailboat. Unfortunately, I found it just about the time the adults decided that we boys and girls were too old to play games that involved hiding in the bushes together in the twilight.

By the time I moved to Oregon, I hadn't seen many of our old neighbors in decades. Some of them were dead, others had moved away, and a few, like my parents, still occupied the same familiar houses of the South Hill. So much time had passed since we were children that most of the days we lived through had been forgotten. Others were indelible, polished and worn like coins and arrowheads of childhood treasure, many involving Margaret and how people treated us because of her.

MICHAELA'S FAMILY, WHO lived up the block, moved to our neighborhood from California when I was in the fifth grade. Michaela's dad taught English at a local community college. I remember thinking there must be something wrong with him, because he didn't scare the crap out of me like dads were supposed to. He was goofy and liked to make his kids laugh. I never saw him wear a tie, either, which made him even harder to take seriously. I once watched with incredulity as he worked a can opener and made us sloppy joes. A cooking dad was something I'd never seen before, like a dancing bear, right there in the kitchen. I wasn't even sure my dad knew where the kitchen was, let alone how the thing worked.

Michaela's mom also "worked outside the home," as they said back then. She always looked really nice and carried a briefcase. I felt sorry for her because she had to go to work instead of staying home as my mom did in her T-shirts and jeans. It never occurred to me that she might have liked her job or that my own mother might have sometimes prayed to Jesus for a professional life that would help her escape a houseful of children.

Whatever the case, these parents were a different breed than I was used to. On the day that the police marched up our front walk, I'd been over at Michaela's house all afternoon. Right before dinner her folks announced that they would walk me home, which struck me as odd. They had never walked me home before, so I figured I must be in some kind of trouble. Nobody walked children home in my neighborhood. (The closest thing for me was being regularly escorted to the front door by one particular mom who had a harder time hiding her irritation with me when it was time to go home.) Back then we ran to and from our friends' houses, morning or evening, and nobody worried about us. Sandy Young and I regularly stood at the pine tree between our houses in the hard dark, one foot on the trunk, and raced each other home, thrilled and terrified to be alone in the darkness, but at the same time knowing we were safe.

Maybe Michaela's parents just wanted to get some exercise, even though this was the eighties, before people knew that exercise was good for you. Whatever the case, there they were, strolling down the hill with their daughter and me on a warm spring evening as if it were something they did every day. That was a Californian for you. They were also holding hands, which made me feel really sorry for Michaela.

Looking back I have to wonder if I said something to make Michaela's parents feel like they should walk me home and see for themselves what was really going on at the Garvin house. It wasn't like me to talk about Margaret's behavior and how it often made me feel like I was roller-skating on a tightrope near the edge of a cliff. It was such a part of my life back then that to talk about it would have seemed as superfluous as telling someone that my family was Irish Catholic—why state the obvious? But maybe when I went to their house that day seeking a little peace and quiet, I happened to mention that someone had called the cops on my sister. *Ha, ha, isn't that funny,* I might have said.

MOST PEOPLE, I imagine, are alarmed by screaming. That's the point, after all; this is how we human beings sound the alarm. The difference between my sister's screaming and the other screaming I've heard since is a measure of quality and quantity. When Margaret had a tantrum, she could hold out for hours.

As a child I spent a lot of time watching her, trying to calm her down, wishing she would stop, but nothing I did seemed to make any difference. I tried comforting her, but often found it difficult to speak in a soothing voice when she was yelling, "AAAAAAAAAAAAAAA AAAAAHHHHHHHHHH! NOOOOOOOOOOO OOOOOOOOOO!" in my face. I felt like I did when a fire engine went by, only this fire engine wasn't going anywhere, so the blaring wasn't getting any quieter. Standing there next to my own personal four-alarm fire, I struggled to figure out how to turn off the siren. I'd alternate between pleading with her to be quiet and yelling at her.

Either way, she couldn't hear me. She'd sit there with her eyes closed, banging her hands and feet against whatever she was standing closest to—the floor, the wall, the furniture, herself—not seeming to feel the pain. The force of her screaming was so great that I expected her uvula to emerge, bringing her esophagus, tonsils, and appendix right along with it. Every once in a while, Margaret would open her eyes and focus on whoever was foolish enough to be in the room with her. Our efforts to calm her usually did not comfort her, and so we were just as likely to become targets for her fists and feet. It was nothing personal; we were just in her space, and when her anxieties took over, we sometimes learned to get the hell out of the way, but often not.

We called these episodes "tantrums," which sounds so benign and friendly. Tantrums were what little kids had when they were whining for ice cream. *Tantrum.* The word has a nice little symphonic ring to it. It sounds like a small piece of Asian percussion, something that would be played during the special music section at Christmas mass. We needed a better word, but we didn't have one, at least not a polite one we could use in front of other people.

Sometimes it was hard to know what had set Margaret off in the first place, but this particular crisis had been about the Blue Goody, a small, cheap, plastic hairbrush with bristles on one side of it. Like so many things in our crowded household, it was the only one of its kind. One hairbrush in a house of seven people. My parents were trying to feed and clothe seven of us, and they were frugal people. So it seemed like there was one of everything in our house: THE hairbrush. THE hammer. THE thermos. This singularity carried a terrible significance: if you broke it, lost it, or failed to share it, forcing your parents to spend $1.06 on a new one at Rosauer's grocery store, you would push the family over the brink of financial disaster and into a breakup of Dickensian proportions. Somehow I managed to believe this mythology even though my father was a senior partner in his obstetrics practice and we owned a lakeside summer home.

But what caused Margaret to start screaming is really

beside the point. Her tantrums were often not connected to anything that the rest of us could understand, even after they were over. She might scream for an entire Saturday afternoon, causing a complete uproar as people either fled, struggled with her, or turned the house upside down looking for whatever object it was that might comfort her—a dog tag in the secret pocket of my mother's purse, the piece of metal from the center of the record player (which she called "the Spindle!"), or the tattered fragment of an album cover. And even when we never found the sought-after object, all of a sudden she could just wind down, take in a shaky breath, and say, "Okay, now. *That's* better." Then she'd go back to whatever it was she had been doing hours before as if nothing had happened. The rest of us would stagger around feeling like there had been a tornado and we were still pulling pieces of roofing and walls off our bodies and prying nails and staples out of our heads and hands.

This is really the clincher. If you yell or cry because you want something or need something or lost something, the people around you want to help. Usually we can help each other, and we take turns comforting each other in this basic way. But if you can't tell anyone what it is that you are screaming bloody murder about, no one has a prayer of helping you. The result is dual alienation. I have no doubt that the origins of my sister's panicked rages were very concrete to her, but because she couldn't explain them to me, there was a wall between us, and we were trapped on our respective sides.

• • •

EVERYBODY IN THE neighborhood knew us, so whoever had called the police had to know that it was Margaret who was causing all the ruckus that day. Frankly, it's a wonder the neighbors didn't call the cops more often. That they didn't made it quite a special occasion to see the men in blue on our block, so I'll bet a lot of people were peeking out through their curtains when the big uniformed officer showed up on our front porch. I know that's what I was doing. I saw the police car pull up to the curb as I stood next to my screaming sister in our bedroom, wondering who was in trouble. Then I realized he was coming to *our* house. I watched him come up the walk, and I pressed my nose against the screen as he disappeared under the eave on our porch. I heard the doorbell ring, and I ran to the top of the stairs to watch my kind, petite mother open the front door. From behind the screen, she tried to explain the situation in her calm, reasonable voice. He let her finish, looked at her like he'd heard it all before, and said something like, "Lady, I have to see for myself." Mom wearily waved him up the stairway to our room, where Margaret had planted herself.

I stood at the top of the stairs watching him climb. It was funny to see a big police officer shouldering his way up the narrow staircase to the second floor of our house, so out of place next to the delicate pencil portraits of our childhood faces in the stairwell. (There were only four; Margaret wouldn't sit still for hers.) He ignored me as he passed, and I followed him into our peach-colored bedroom with frilly curtains and matching bedspreads, all hand sewn by my mother. Margaret was sitting on one of our twin beds, quiet for the moment and sweating. Clearly this didn't look like a den of iniquity and torture. It looked like a little girl's room. My mother came into the room and stood behind him and told Margaret that the nice man was worried about her. And then the nice man went over to where she was sitting to ask her if she was okay. He said something like, "Honey, are you okay? Are you hurt? Can you tell me what happened?"

After a moment of silence, Margaret took a deep breath and looked at him. Then she reared back, grabbed a fistful of bedspread in each hand, and howled in his face: "WHEREEEEEEEEE ISSSSSSSSSSSSSSSS THE BLUUUUUUUUUUUUE HAAAAAIR-RRRRRRRRBRUUUUUUUUUUUSH! I DON'T KNOW WHERE IT IS! DO YOU WANT THE BLUE HAIRBRUSH? AAAAAAAAHHHHHH! AAAAAAAAHHHHH!" Then she threw herself backward on the bed, kicking her legs and thrashing around. The policeman fled, his white face a blur as he rushed by me in the doorway. Clearly he had been convinced that there was no law to be enforced here. I gave up, too, and went up to Michaela's house. Later in the afternoon she and her parents escorted me home.

Were Michaela's parents coming to look at my family's demons that day? Were they were luridly curious, genuinely concerned, or just being friendly? Whatever the case, I remember that it was nearing twilight as we headed down Wall Street. Walking in front with Michaela, I felt oddly formal with the adults in tow as we approached the front of my house. Perhaps that's why I went to the front door, the same one the policeman had gone to, the one that the rest of us never used. I knew it would be locked, but instead of going around to the side door, where I knew my family would be gathered in front of the TV, I reached out and poked the doorbell, just like the cop had.

My mother came to the front of the house and opened the screen door, met Michaela's parents, and charmed them like she charmed everyone. Margaret, worn out from her afternoon of anxiety, came and stood behind her. At thirteen she was already taller than my mother. She wrapped one arm lovingly around our mother's neck, smelled the back of her head, and rested her forehead on Mom's shoulder. She watched Michaela's parents and watched my mother, and I watched all of them. Every once in a while, Margaret would interject something like, "You don't scream about the blue hairbrush, Mom." Or, "That's good being quiet now, Mom." And my mother would agree with her. "Yes, Margaret. That is good behaving."

After they had chatted for a time, Michaela's parents said good night and walked up the hill in the dark toward their house. I went in the house, my mother shut the door, and we all sat down for dinner. The next day at school Michaela told me that when they got home that night, her parents had taken down the For Sale sign that they had recently put up in the front yard and went inside. She said she didn't know why. They didn't move back to California. And the next time my mom went to the store, we got a new hairbrush. A brown Goody, with bristles all the way around.

THE PAST ISN'T singular, a large block of was or wasn't, did or didn't, had or hadn't. It includes many layers compressed over the years. Memory, ours and others, is accurate and misremembered, abandoned and reclaimed. It is like stone itself. If you cut a cross section, you can read the floods and the droughts, years of famine or plenty. In my own cross section I found marks made by these friends and neighbors I'd almost forgotten. And after all that time, I found some of what hadn't been said to be what I treasured the most.

In Oregon these days were long past from my life, the times when something as inconsequential as a misplaced hairbrush could cause enough of a crisis to marshal my family, the neighbors, and the Spokane Police Department to the same hopeless cause. But for years after I left home, I still lived in the shadow of the other shoe, waiting for some small disruption to swing the balance and make it drop, make the normal life I had struggled so hard to build fall apart in an instant. I felt this way even when I was old enough to know that people have to deal with their own demons, their own crying babies and screaming little girls.

Even Margaret. For all of our efforts, I can't believe

we ever really helped my sister find any peace of mind. Margaret held the key that eluded the rest of us, and when she was able to open the door and return to the regular world, she did it of her own accord, not because of anything we did or didn't do to help her. When I saw her that first summer after I moved to Oregon, I was more certain of that than anything. I could see that she continued to struggle with the same kinds of things every day, but I knew there was less tumultuousness in her life, and I was happy for her, because she deserved peace of mind more than anyone I knew.

From my old neighborhood, my life moved on: Spokane, Seattle, England, American Samoa, Spain, New Mexico. I watched people come and go from my life, and talismans helped me remember. When I got married, Deanna and Vanessa gave me my own candy jar as a shower gift, generously stuffed with my favorite sweets. I brought that memory of my childhood into my first married home. By the time Margaret first came to visit me there in Albuquerque, the jar had been broken, elbowed off the counter by my lanky husband, who didn't think I would notice its absence if he didn't say anything about it. I cried for hours. But lots of things got broken there, and everywhere else I lived. Like the Blue Goody hairbrush, though, these things are nothing more than plastic and glass—replaceable and inconsequential when compared to our memories and the people in our lives, who we struggle to love and be loved by, with their imperfections and through our own.

Sometimes sitting on my porch at night in Oregon, I could hear the frog families croaking across the fence line, the sound of a lone dog barking once, twice, three times. Across the river I heard the whistle of the train as it sped along the Columbia River Gorge, moving east toward Spokane and ever forward in time. I heard the voices of neighborhood children calling to each other across their yards in the darkness. I remembered what I had had before and what I had still, and I held it all in the unbreakable jar of my heart.

8.

the know-nothing aunt

Often we save our best manners for company and even
for strangers, giving less than our best to our families
and friends. How unfortunate that is, since these are the
relationships that matter most in our lives.

—*On Relationships,* EMILY POST'S ETIQUETTE

I COULDN'T SLEEP, PARTLY because I was in a strange bed. From a horizontal vantage point on the hide-a-bed in my sister Ann's living room, I lay awake for hours gazing at framed pictures, carved wooden figurines, and shapely Asian ceramic bowls—the trappings of a life that had taken Ann from a small town in Washington State to Germany and then the Mojave Desert and Boston and China and back to the United States again. I was thinking about the work it must have taken to haul these items from place to place as the U.S. Army moved her family around so frequently over the past two decades. Even though they had been living in this particular house for only a couple of months, this stuff was there, hammered and hung, measured and straightened, looking like it had never been anywhere else. I wondered if Ann looked at these items as a way to mark her place in the world, the touchstones she'd carefully collected to make herself at home no matter where on the globe she might be. Or maybe it's just a bunch of crap that she hauls around out of habit and that she secretly wishes would get lost or damaged in the move.

As I lay there not sleeping, ruminating on her family's travels, I was also thinking about how having children seems to make people's guest rooms disappear. Suddenly all the bedrooms are chock-full of children. There is no sleeping space for visiting adults, so people like me get stuck out on the couch or some air mattress in the middle of the house while the children are all snuggled up in their private suites with extra pillows and the luxury of a door that closes. I'd driven three hundred miles that afternoon and was hoping for—no, expecting—a room of my own. I felt a bit like an old crone for thinking such things, but I also felt a bit like I'd been left out on the lawn with the sprinkler and scattered toys: Exposed. Neglected. Stepped on.

The soft mattress under me slanted down at the top, which made all the blood in my body rush toward my head. This was an uncomfortable sensation, to say the least, not to mention the fact that I could feel each horizontal steel bar beneath me. However, I had convinced myself that my position was probably not dangerous, unless my head slid farther down into the crease between the mattress and the back of the couch, causing the hide-a-bed to suddenly engage and put itself away. But I was trying not to let myself think about that sort of thing.

Mostly I couldn't sleep because there was a pair of seven-year-old feet lodged in the middle of my spine. The feet belonged to my carrot-haired nephew, Tony, who had asked his mother if he could sleep in the hide-a-bed—what he called the Big Nana Pat Bed—with Auntie Eileen. She hadn't actually cleared this request with me. She had just mentioned it with a smile and went to tuck him in, leaving me standing in the kitchen wondering to myself if there is a polite way to tell a seven-year-old that you don't relish his nocturnal company. Turns out there isn't. Besides, by the time I went to bed, Tony had been asleep for hours. Now here he was, snoring gently into my ear and digging his little toes into my road-weary back.

My nephew is an adorable little person. It's just that I have long had a strong aversion to sharing a bed with anyone; even Brendan barely made the cut. As a child I was forced to share a room with two sisters until the oldest one, this kid's mom, Ann, went away to college. That left Margaret and me bunking together for another five years until I left for school. Even after all this time, I still jealously guard my own space. When traveling with a large group of my girlfriends, I'd happily sleep on the floor before volunteering to share a bed.

the know-nothing aunt

When they asked why, I tried to explain that I didn't like to be looked at when I was sleeping. People told me that this was a rather ridiculous fear, because when people sleep together they are sleeping, not looking at each other. But those people never had to share a room with Margaret.

BEING WATCHED IN my sleep—it's a worry I had nurtured nightly through the eighteen years I shared a room with my autistic sister, this kid's other aunt, who was three years my senior and seemed to never sleep. She had disrupted my rest for nearly two decades with her nocturnal wanderings and strange whisperings. I often awoke to the sound of her feet thundering down the stairs to check on something, as she was wont to do in her compulsive and unpredictable nighttime travels. My older brothers and I would try to police this kind of activity, because we didn't want her to wake up our dad, who was sleep deprived during the entire course of his career as an obstetrician and would come roaring up the stairs in that signature, Scary Dad in Underwear way that men of his generation had perfected. If he awoke, we were doomed.

Therefore, if one of us heard Margaret getting out of bed, we'd all leap up to chase her. Consequently, Margaret developed a habit of running and slamming doors behind her as she went, because she knew someone would be hot on her heels trying to get her to go back to bed. Even if we didn't chase her, when we'd long given up on this tactic, she'd run and slam because she'd gotten used to doing so: *Slap! Slam! Slam! Wham! Wham! Wham! Wham!* Her feet would hit the floor and she'd be out of bed, through two doors, down the stairs, through the living room, into the kitchen, and back again. As she thundered back up the stairs to the second floor, where we kids slept, I'd hear my mother's quiet scolding, "Margaret, now, you go to bed!" Sometimes this was, in fact, my mother following Margaret up the stairs to make sure she went back to bed. But sometimes Margaret would rush back up the stairs on her own, scolding herself in a perfect imitation of our mother's voice, saving Mom the trouble of getting out of bed. It was kind of like Gilligan hitting himself with Skipper's hat when he knew he'd done something dumb.

Weekend mornings were worse, when I tried to make up for lost sleep. Margaret would roll out of bed much earlier than I did, anxiety propelling her into her clothes and down the stairs to the kitchen. And there she'd pace, waiting for the rest of us to follow her so that she could begin another daylong session of record playing from the eclectic family collection. Bay City Rollers. Electric Light Orchestra. Roger Whittaker. *Carmina Burana.* There was little peace to be had in a house with five children living in it, and my sister's habits just increased the sense of chaos. Even so, our mother did what she could to set some kind of boundary with the records. Margaret was allowed to turn on her music, "When the other kids get up."

Of course, as I've said before, waiting for anything was very difficult for Margaret. Her anxiety-fueled pacing and talking to my mother shook the walls and rattled the doorknobs, but, to be fair, the music stayed off. Sometimes I'd lie there listening to her ask my mother, "You're going to play the music, Mom?" and my mother would answer, "When the other kids get up." I'd hear Margaret walk away and sit on the couch with a thump, and about ten seconds would pass before she'd get up, hurry into the kitchen, and ask, "You're going to play the music, Mom?" My mother would repeat the same answer, cheerfully, endlessly it seemed.

"When the other kids get up, then you can play the music, Margaret."

"When the other kids get up, *then* you can play the music, Mom."

"That's right, Margs."

"*Then* you can play the music."

"Then you can play the music, Margs."

"*Then* you can play the music, Mom."

"Then you can play the music, Margs."

After a certain period of time, Margaret just couldn't stand it anymore. She'd sprint into the kitchen and switch on the stereo at full volume for a split second, blasting music through the house. Before someone yelled at her to turn it down, she had already turned it off again. Of course I was no longer sleeping after that, but I clung stubbornly to my right to be in bed, and I kept my eyes shut tight. Often, Margaret would start checking on me to see if I was moving. I'd pretend like I was asleep as she pounded up the stairs and shuffled to my bedside. Then she'd just stand there, breathing on me. I'd look at her through my lashes, always sensing that she knew I was faking my slumber.

Some days her face would be pulled into lines of worry, and she'd stand there twisting her hands, looking like she was about to cry or scream. On other days I would see her mischievous smile. "You can play the music when the kids get up," she'd say loudly, into my face. And if I so much as flickered an eyelash, she'd pounce on me, rolling around on the bed and laughing, "YOU'RE GOING TO LISTEN TO THE MUSIC WHEN EILEEN GETS UP! HA HA HA HA!" Then she'd sprint down the stairs to crank up the stereo. "You're going to listen to the music when Eileen gets up, Mom!" she'd holler up from the kitchen in her high monotone voice. And I'd be, against my will, up.

I've never quite recovered from those days. I still hide my face in the morning, only now I'm hiding from my dog, who starts pawing at my shoulder if she sees me move, hoping to expedite a quicker breakfast. I feign sleep around the cats, one of which starts knocking pictures off the walls or flinging my glasses and other bedside items if she thinks there's a chance I'll rise up and open the window for her, the other one wanting me to fill her very

special water bowl in the bathroom and crying and pacing
if she sees me awake. Yes, it's true—I'm a grown woman
who feels the need to deceive her pets. But I hide from my
husband, too, who, like Margaret, always wants to get up
early on the weekends. So far, he has been easier to fool
with the pretending-to-be-asleep bit.

ALL OF THIS is to say that sleep-related anxiety makes me
pretty keen to avoid shared sleeping arrangements. If I
sleep alone, I don't have to worry about being watched
or, consequently, try to hide the fact that I am worried
about it. But no such luck this time. Here I was, trapped
by the enthusiasm of a sweet young boy. As I lay awake,
I knew I should be flattered by the attention. At least I
wasn't some scary relative that everyone hid from—the
Aunt with the Hairy Mole, the Aunt Who Chews with
Her Mouth Open, the Aunt with the BO Who Hugs
Way Too Much. Tony was young enough to take it for
granted that he liked me just because I was his auntie.
He was too young to make any critical sort of judg-
ment about me as a person; I was just an aunt. For this I
knew I should be grateful. I took a deep breath and tried
to focus on gratitude, but I moved in the wrong direction and felt a muscle in my lower back start to spasm.
While I waited for the pain to pass, it occurred to me
that there weren't too many years left for Tony to be so
cuddly. As the youngest of my sister's three kids, he toler-
ated the babying, snuggling, and hand-holding. But his
big brother was on the football team, his dad was in the

military, and I knew a time was coming when the little man in him wouldn't stand for any of it; he'd rise up and throw off the sweet bonds of women's affection, at least while other people were looking.

As I finished this thought, Tony kicked me in his sleep and my spine twanged like a loosely strung violin. My sleeplessness intensified, and I realized that in just a few short hours I was going to have to face a room full of alert family members, and I was pretty sure there wasn't any coffee in the house. This thought terrified me into full wakefulness. I thought about climbing the stairs into Tony's room and taking over his twin bed so that I would get enough sleep to communicate with my relatives long enough to find out where the nearest coffee shop was. Then a powerful thought came to me and superseded the caffeine problem. *I'm never going to have one of these,* I thought. *I'll never have a little boy of my own.* Suddenly I felt completely calm and aware. I don't have any children, and it's unlikely that I ever will. I often ponder the advantages of this decision, but at that moment, as Tony pitched onto his side and threw me an elbow, all I could think of was the loss it brought. The realization pierced me sharply just then, and the little feet didn't bother me anymore, and after a while I fell asleep.

The reason I was in the Big Nana Pat Bed in the first place was that I was on an aunt errand, one I probably wouldn't have been able to perform if I'd had kids of my own, in fact. Ann, whose husband was out of the country, had asked me to stay with her three children—Bobby, Julia, and Tony—while she attended a class in another town. My mission was simple: pick the little kids up from school, be home when Bobby got home from carpool, feed them dinner, make sure they did their homework, and keep them alive until they left for school the next morning. Then I was off the hook. I had accepted, but with a pang of fear in my heart. As a childless freelance writer, I lead a rather simple life. My day is centered on the coffeepot and a hot shower. I wander around in my bathrobe for the better part of the morning, and if you took away my computer and replaced it with a television, people watching what I do all day would say "loser" instead of "writer." It's all relative. Despite the simplicity of my solitary routine, I can make a part-time job out of letting the cats in and out on a given day. Being responsible for humans was another matter entirely. But I wanted to do it, so I had said yes and tried to feel brave.

For an hour or so after I arrived at their house, I just stood in the middle of the kitchen, wide-eyed. *Living with children must make you feel like your house is haunted,* I thought. Around every corner of Ann's house was the sound of a person, or a pile of that person's stuff, a recently vacated chair sliding across the floor, an electronic device just turned on, the shadow of a child disappearing around a corner, the flash of a shirttail, a sock heel. It seemed like they were in constant motion, so I stood still, clutched my glass of wine, and tried to pay attention to the directions my sister was giving while she made dinner. She'd get about halfway through some complex explanation about their education, health care, or spiritual well-being, and then she'd look up at me and say, "Oh, you know what I'm talking about." I was too overwhelmed to say, "Do I? Are you sure?"

As we sat together enjoying the meal she'd prepared, my confusion intensified. It seemed like they all talked at the same time, but that could have been the wine. My sister mediated the conversation by asking each of them to tell the rest of us three things they'd done that day. Bobby was taking his turn when I heard Tony making a funny noise, and when I looked at him I realized he was choking. Before I could even think of what to do, he opened his mouth to breathe. A warm mist of milk sprayed across the table and showered my hair, shoulders, and chest. I sat there, milky beads cascading down the wales of my corduroy shirt, not reacting. There was a moment of silence, and then they all dissolved with laughter, my sister laughing the loudest. The four of them pounded on the table and gasped for air, unable to speak. I reached up with my napkin and dabbed at the milk pooling in my collarbone, calmly patted my hair, and waited for them to be quiet. After a minute or two it occurred to me that it really was hilarious to have milk in my hair, and I started to chuckle, which made them laugh harder. Then I really got going and snorted so loud that Tony nearly spewed milk all over me again. Eventually we pulled ourselves together and finished dinner. Thank God there was a parent there to lead us through.

• • •

IT'S TIMES LIKE this when I feel like my emotional comprehension runs about two minutes behind everyone else's. And when you think about the nuances of humor, grief, or anger, that's a lot of time. This lag time was kind of trained into me as a kid, when I had spent years trying not to respond to some antic of my sister's. For instance, Margaret always got a huge kick out of spitting her juice in our faces at the dinner table. Some of her jokes would come and go after a few days or weeks, like chin pinching or hair pulling, but this one stuck around for years. As we five kids sat crowded around our sticky dining room table, one of us would feel the weight of her eyes upon us and, unwillingly, turn to look at her. She'd blow like a spouting whale, just inches away. Then she'd laugh and laugh, and our mother would tell us not to react, because it would only encourage her to do it more. So we'd just sit there with water or juice running down our cheeks and take another bite of canned corn or beans while she loaded up and did it all over again. Sometimes I'd get angry and yell at her, which usually made her laugh harder, and she'd say something like, "You don't spit your juice, Eileen! That's good manners! Ha ha ha ha ha!" And then she would spit on me again. She also loved to grab the gallon jug of milk out of the refrigerator and pour it down the drain to make us scream, "No, Margaret! Don't pour the milk out!" This also made her laugh, and we were not supposed to respond as she hollered, "You don't pour the milk out! Ha! Ha! Ha!"

We've spent a lot of time not reacting to Margaret's kooky jokes, and I don't think it has made a bit of difference. I love her and she has shaped my life in ways that I continue to try to understand, but when I was young, mostly I felt like I wanted to kill her when she did this sort of thing. In college when I read the myth of Sisyphus, I felt an immediate kinship. I knew what it was like to do the same thing over and over again, to go beyond exhaustion with the repetition of some meaningless task, and to wake up the next day and do it all over again without any hope of reprieve. That's how I felt when we, as a family, were trying to teach Margaret to do, or not do, something. I always think about Margaret when I am around other people's children, because I was one of the many people who helped bring her up. Although I am three years younger than she, I am, for all intents and purposes, her big sister, and it's the only frame of reference I have for child rearing. I realize it is not a conservative comparison, but it's all I've got.

Tony, unlike Margaret, only spit on me the one time. And I came to recognize that it was an accident, although after the response he got, you could tell he really wanted to do it again. After Ann left for her class, I kept reminding myself that these three children were not like my unpredictable sister. They were fairly reasonable little people; they had rules and a moral code. They might have been a bit too focused on keeping score—who ate the last cookie, whose turn it was for Xbox, who got to pick the last movie—but at least they all followed the same basic playbook with a range of rules: What Is Allowed, What Is Not Allowed, and What Aunt Eileen Might Not Know Is Not Allowed. This last category left me at a serious disadvantage. The rules and regulations of the childhood code of ethics seemed to have left me, and I felt panicked. I thought I was supposed to have some kind of answer to their nonstop negotiating for sugary snacks, television, a later bedtime, or their turn with a toy. The internal bickering and massive power struggles made me feel like Colin Powell during the Bush administration: I was supposed to have the answers, but no one was listening to me.

But I soon realized that I didn't have to say much, if anything at all. These kids knew what was right and wrong within the family charter, even if I didn't. I found that if I didn't say anything and just looked knowingly at them, they came to the answer on their own. This tactic kept the peace and gave the illusion, at least, that I was on to them.

To be fair, they didn't give me any real trouble, because they are good kids. They've moved around in the migratory army life—California, Massachusetts, Virginia, Beijing, Virginia again, Hong Kong, Virginia one last time, and now Washington State. Through all that, they've hung together. They are kind to one another and still play together, even the boys, who are separated by seven years.

And did they ever play; this was a gaming family. On the first night the three of them tried to teach me to play chess, a game I have never even tried, but which is a passion for my husband. It made me shudder, the anonymous-looking pieces and the blank board, which somehow inspired very mysterious, specific moves. Where were the chutes and ladders? The Lollipop Forest? The metal wheelbarrow and Scotty dog? But Bobby, Tony, and Julia were good little teachers. Plus we were using the *Lord of the Rings* chess set with its recognizable Orcs and Wizards and such, not those neutered-looking wooden pegs. I was actually starting to catch on, and then I won by default when Tony, who had been beating me soundly, fell victim to teasing from his older brother, got pissed off, and threw the board.

On the second night, they asked me what I wanted to play after dinner, and I said, "What do you have?" "Risk," they said, "and Murder in the Abbey, and Scattergories, and Cranium." I said I didn't know how to play any of those, but I'd be willing to learn.

Tony slapped the table with an open palm like he'd just about had it with me. "Aunt Eileen, you don't know ANYTHING!" he exclaimed. The older kids looked at me to see if I was going to get mad. I'm pretty sure there is a rule in the family charter about how you are supposed to address adults, but by this time I'd decided that I mostly fall into the middle ground regarding this sort of etiquette; I am not a parent and I am not a child, but I feel a closer kinship to the children, especially when I'm sleeping on the hide-a-bed in the middle of the living room. So I just smiled at Tony and told him it was okay that I didn't know anything, because I had him to teach me.

That's the truth, too. These kids taught me something every time I saw them. I learned not to be terrified if Julia asked me to brush her beautiful auburn hair in the morning. I used to flee the comb myself, and remembering the unkind pull of the sharp teeth in my own snarly young locks, I was afraid I would hurt her. But this kid was resilient. I brushed, I braided, and I wasn't half bad at it. She smiled at me and told me I did a pretty good job.

With Tony I learned to trust that I would know what to say when he padded into the kitchen at 10:00 PM in his little Spiderman pajamas to tell me he couldn't sleep. That I would find some trick in my Auntie Toolbox to comfort him enough so that he'd be able to slide into bed and burrow his head down like a small animal, wearing the remnant of his security blanket like a scarf. And he showed me I can get over my ancient hang-ups—like sharing a bed with somebody else and not minding if I don't sleep very well.

And then there was Bobby, the stoic eldest. When I went to bed and saw his light on upstairs, I thought about his lonely breakfast that morning in the dark kitchen. He had to leave at 7:00 AM each day for high school in the next town over and at fourteen was getting himself up and out the door on his own. I worried that I had been too serious about following my sister's instructions about the rules. So I got out of bed and climbed up the stairs. I poked my head in through his open door and saw Bobby with his headphones on, doing his homework. I pointed at the clock and called him the family vampire. That made him smile. We talked about how fun it is to stay up late and how hard it is to get up in the morning. He told me about what he was working on, a critique for his creative writing class. I didn't say much. I didn't know what to say, but I just wanted him to know that I saw him, that I recognized him, and that I could see the person he is always becoming.

The next morning I listened to Bobby trying to get up for an hour—5:45 AM, 6:00 AM, 6:15 AM, 6:30 AM—his alarm shouting me awake every fifteen minutes. *Alarm!* Snooze. *Alarm!* Snooze. I dragged myself into the kitchen to make some coffee at 7:00 AM and told him he should get a medal for getting up so early. Before he left, I put my arms around him and told him to come visit me in Oregon soon.

Julia and Tony held my hands on the way to school, and I loved the feeling of their smooth little paws. More than that, I loved the feeling of trust, their cheerful assumption that I love them back, which I do, immensely. They let go of me and jumped up to walk the rock wall next to the sidewalk, all the while chatting away to me, not missing a step. At the school I watched them head into their separate classrooms and into a day that would become part of a lifetime as it piled up on the other days that had come before it. And I hoped my short time with them would be a good memory in that pile.

I DROVE HOME through the Pacific Northwest rain, dodging semitrucks and puddles, thinking of their red-gold hair, their sweet faces, their laughter. I thought about my sister and her husband, the architects of their children's characters. *How do you do it?* I wondered. How do you figure out the right rules to sustain you through a day, a year, or a lifetime? When do you know you are teaching them how to become the people they were born to be and when you are getting in their way? Is it the success of the day-to-day or the crisis that proves it to you? How do you encourage them to do things their own way, and how do you stand back and let them fail, knowing that it is just one small part of who they will become?

Soon I was back in my quiet house with my needy cats and my patient dog. Nobody wanted to play with me. They just wanted food, water, and the couch. After climbing the stairs that night, I was happy to be in my own bed, but I missed the warmth and weight of Tony dreaming next to me. My house was full of the dark and the silence that comes from the absence of children. And even after all these years, I still felt the quiet created by Margaret's absence.

I knew then that having Margaret as a sister played some part in my decision not to have children. It's not that I was worried about giving birth to a child with disabilities. The odds are against it. And the rational part of me knew that raising a non-autistic child wouldn't be as difficult. A child could learn and grow and change in ways that might seem like magic to me after watching Margaret struggle to learn the kinds of things we take for granted: Look at people when you talk to them; eat your food in small bites, get dressed before you come out of the locker room, don't spank Father Bach or run a fingertip up ladies' pantyhose on the way back from communion. My mother, Margaret's teachers, and countless others worked with her over the years and so did the rest of us family members. There was so much that she could never master, and in trying to help teach her, I had always felt like I was failing over and over again.

It was not rational, but I knew it was part of the reason I'd chosen not to be a parent. I wouldn't ever know what my life would have been like if I had made a different choice, but that was something I had to live with, just as we all live with our choices.

There was so much I didn't know. I still didn't know how to play chess, and I didn't care if I ever did. I didn't know what it took to raise a child to feel loved and safe and independent. I didn't know what Margaret's life was really like, if she was happy, if she thought of me. I'd often wished I could have found more reserves of humor and laughter for her, for me, when we were sharing a house. I tried to remember when I first got the notion that I was responsible for her behavior and for her future. I asked myself if all that time I thought I was working so hard to help her had made any difference at all. I wondered if I had really done anything at all besides worry. Some of these were questions I was not sure I wanted to know the answers to.

There were a few things I did know. I was pretty sure I'd never be a mother, but I also knew what it was to be an aunt and a sister, and that meant a great deal to me. I loved watching my sister and her husband succeed at this important task. I was also beginning to realize that our lives are our own to shape and heal as well as we are able. If we are lucky, we have people we love and call family. As for my siblings, I was learning to hope that I could have adult relationships with each of them now that we lived closer. And I had decided to try to let go of my expectations about what those relationships should be like. I'd decided to just see what would happen. As for all those things that remained mysterious and unknown, I could only hope that I would be paying attention if the answers ever revealed themselves.

That night, I lay in bed, not sleeping in my quiet house. Outside I could hear the eternal wind of the Columbia River Gorge rushing over the peak of the roof and squealing around the corner eaves. I closed my eyes and listened to the whistling dark. And then I was falling toward sleep, holding the two of them, Margaret and Tony, in my mind's eye: Here is Margaret, rushing through the dark hallway in her flannel nightgown like the wind itself, gripping a tattered record cover in one hand and scolding herself in a whisper. And here is Tony, muttering in his sleep, clutching his tattered baby blanket to his chest.

I saw them and I saw the truth. We hold so tightly to what we treasure, not knowing that grasping what is precious to us only makes it fall away faster, not realizing that if we would loosen our hold, the objects of our affections would become lighter than the air we breathe, more magical than our dreams, more constant than sleep. And in that we can find rest.

9.

what's next, margaret?

If you cannot participate in sports or games with grace
and good temper, you should not participate at all.
Cursing your luck, excusing, complaining and protesting
against unfairness won't get you anywhere.

—*On Being a Good Sport*, EMILY POST'S ETIQUETTE

ON A PERFECT June morning I stood in the sunlight in my front yard, hose in hand, watering the berm I'd recently planted on the west side of my lawn. Since I'd moved to Oregon, gardening had given me a sense of pleasure I never knew was possible. How satisfying to plan, to clear a space, and to plant small, delicate seedlings. To begin. What a surprise to watch these small green shoots grow and blossom, even thrive. I was happy I hadn't give up on gardening after my first attempt, which amounted to nothing short of seedling slaughter. I was living in New Mexico at the time, and it had never occurred to me that soil and climate had much to do with the mass destruction that had followed my first attempts. I'd always thought it was me.

I'd been thinking about beginnings a lot. Not so much first attempts as much as second tries and second chances. I'd never been much good at sticking with something unless it was easy at first. I was used to things coming easily—academics, sports, music—or not at all. Now here I was in my fourth decade starting all over with all kinds of things—activities and work and relationships—inconceivable as that might have seemed just a few years ago.

I was thinking about all of this as I moved my hose across the berm, spraying across the hopeful faces of blue fescue, bright yarrow, thready Karl Foerster grass, lavender. I was cheered, inexplicably, by the wind stirring the diminutive branches of the miniature tabletop pine I had planted for Brendan. I had spent hours clearing the weeds from this spot, working the soil, choosing the plants, plotting the layout, laying weed cloth, shoveling mulch. And all of a sudden, there it was, just like I pictured it would be. How satisfying and how unusual.

To date, my life had not been as tidy as this little plot of land. I had grown up with the dynamics of autism, so I was used to surprises, but I was unaccustomed to the happy ending. I was hardwired for the quirky finale, the crisis, and the climax of the unforeseen and the unmanageable. Even though I hadn't lived with my sister for almost twenty years, when it came to Margaret, I always expected the worst. That gloomy outlook had somehow bled over into my daily life years ago, giving me an incredible imagination for disaster. First out of habit and then out of talent, I'd spent a lot of time imagining things going terribly wrong, things that have never actually happened: car accidents, fires, fistfights, general crime and mayhem. Every time Brendan was five minutes late, I was sure the state patrol was pulling his car out of the icy slough. When the cat wouldn't come in at night, it was a rabid raccoon that got her. When the plane hit a patch of turbulence, it was all I could do not to clutch the hand of the stranger sitting next to me and tell her about the things I hold dearest in this life.

I'd been trying to give up this habit. It just wasn't very restful. Plus, the rational side of me knew that there really are people who live in crisis day in and day out and that I should count my blessings that I was no longer one of them.

As I watered my colorful garden, I thought about a pending trip home to see my sister and admitted to myself how nervous I was about the things I couldn't predict. I'd put this trip off month after month without a good reason. But I was pretty sure it was mostly because I didn't know what would happen when I got there. I knew what might happen: I could drive three hundred miles to her house just to have her slam the door in my face. This hadn't happened for a long time, but it was still a very real possibility.

IT HAD BEEN more than six months since I had last seen Margaret and gone hiking with her. At first the winter kept me away; icy roads climbing out of the Columbia River Gorge and up into the desert plains of eastern Washington were too much for my two-wheel drive and my nerves. But the snow had melted a long time ago, and now what was keeping me was just the uncertainty. Six months is a long time to go without seeing someone, and yet with Margaret, it might seem the same as six days or six years. I didn't know what she thought about time. For her, five minutes could seem like an eternity when she had to wait. And yet she might greet me after several months as if she had just seen me the day before. Because her communication skills were so limited, we didn't correspond, at least not in a normal way. I'd send a postcard every now and then. Sometimes I would call and talk to a staff member about how she was doing. At the end of our conversation they'd hand the phone to Margaret, who usually said hello before hanging up on me. As a result, there were large drifts of silence between our visits.

But it wasn't like we would have months of catching up to do, either. Margaret didn't talk much, so I antici-pated that when I did see her there would be a lot of quiet, maybe some sudden singing or loud commentary. Or whispering behind her cupped hand. If I wanted to know how she had been, I had to ask her caregivers, the people who were paid to make sure she ate three meals a day, took a shower, brushed her teeth, got to swimming practice, and left the locker room with her swimsuit turned around the right way. These people were almost complete strangers to me, and yet they inhabited my sister's daily life and created the stability she needed just as my family used to.

If I asked Margaret how she'd been, she wouldn't be able to tell me. She wouldn't be able to ask me, either. I doubted she even knew what any of that meant in the context that we normally ask each other these kinds of questions: Tell me what you've been thinking and feeling. How are your old wounds, and do you have any new ones? What about your joys? So we wouldn't have any long conversation like some sisters might. We would just have the day—a car ride, a hike, lunch, the drive home—things we both enjoy. We'd just have those few hours to spend together—mostly in silence—and maybe that was enough.

At the time, I had been very conscious of her absence in my life. I didn't miss the bad times, the years of family tension and violent outbursts—years that I had spent feeling somehow simultaneously responsible and resentful, ineffective and unappreciated. Countless times Margaret had worked herself into a rage or a panic over some nameless thing that she couldn't communicate. And there was absolutely nothing to be done but wait it out, like one waits for a cyclone to pass. But we struggled against it anyway, trying to calm her down; trying to get her to stop throwing herself on the floor, against walls; trying to tame the screaming with our own quiet words, our own anger and tears of impotence. Those years were like battle, and they cast a shadow far into our twenties and thirties.

Walking on the beach in Mexico at Christmas, my brother Mike had told me about the emotional turbulence a friend of his was going through. "Yes," I said. "I've been depressed before, too. It was really, really hard." Mike nodded. "But it only lasted about twenty years," I said. And then we both just howled. Perhaps it had taken this long for the quiet to take hold, for the dust to settle, for me to feel Margaret's absence in my life.

I missed my sister. I felt the lack of her very physical presence. I missed her familiar bulk, the feel of her thin hand in mine when she was happy, the sound of her joyful laugh, her real, beautiful smile, not the fake one she saved for the camera. If I closed my eyes, I saw Margaret in a red-and-white-striped shirt and blue jeans with an elastic waistband, white tennis shoes—her teenage uniform. She had a bob and bangs, like me, our eternal haircut. I breathed in this image and smelled spaghetti noodles, one of her favorite foods. She often spilled food on herself from eating too quickly. This wasn't an unpleasant smell, although I was often embarrassed for her. But I got used to the stains on the front of her shirts, got used to helping my mother pick out "Margaret-colored clothes" that didn't show the food stains as prominently. And later, when I was in graduate school and my friend Anne gestured to her own large breasts and referred to them as "the crumb shelf," I thought of my well-endowed sister and laughed. Maybe Margaret wasn't so strange after all.

When we were children, Margaret smelled like flowers, moist and powdered after her nighttime bath. She'd swoop around the bedroom in her long cotton nightgown and bare feet. She'd race laughing up the stairs, the family dog yipping with excitement and nipping at her hem, as she shouted, "I be the winner!" She'd collapse in hilarity on her twin bed in the room we shared. When I was in college and we were in our twenties, she was still doing this. These times were better than the bad times—the times when her wailing could last for hours, drawing the neighbors and even the police to our door.

I could remember the feel of her skinny arms wrapped around me as she crushed me into her big, soft belly, cackling at some joke of her own making. Margaret would hug me so hard she'd pull me off of my feet. She would also reach around and yank me up by the neck as if I were weightless. But Margaret hadn't hugged me like that in years. Nor had she spanked me, pinched me, whacked me on top of the head, or spit on me like she'd used to. When I was home, I no longer walked around the kitchen with my ass to the wall, forever on defense against some silent but inevitable attack. When she was being her noisy self, our father called her Thunderfoot, and yet when she wanted to sneak up on one of us, she had the stealth of a Jedi Knight. But not anymore.

The minutes and hours and days we spent trying to get her to behave, to stop doing the things we didn't want her to do, were piled up in a closet of our past, gathering dust like her old records in my parents' basement. It was all meaningless now, though at the time it seemed like scolding her and trying to redirect her behavior was all we did. Trying to be reasonable myself, I might say, "Please don't hit me, Margaret. That hurts when you do that, and I know you have good manners." Or in a less composed moment, I might clutch my head and say something like, "God DAMN it, Margaret! Don't fucking hit me!" She'd just laugh and parrot back, "You don't hit me! Ha! Ha! Ha!" and then she'd raise her hand to pretend like she was going to do it again and then laugh some more and run away.

Sometimes she tried to behave. I could tell she was trying. And we really tried to think through how to help her understand what we were asking of her. As a teenager, Mike once sat at the table calmly explaining to Margaret why it just isn't nice to spit on people, especially to spit *your* dinner on them when they are eating *their* dinner. The spitting phase was just bugging the shit out of everybody, and he was trying to make her understand. Margaret sat there and appeared to be listening to our brother like a totally reasonable person. She put on a serious face, said "Okay, Mike," and nodded as though she agreed with him completely that it was a really good idea if she used her polite table manners from now on. Then she took a big gulp of her soda, held it in her cheeks, and erupted in laughter, showering Mike with sugary drink. Mike just closed his eyes, wiped his face with his T-shirt, and left the table without a word. Once during the spitting phase he and our brother Larry tried another tactic—spraying their own drinks back in her face. She thought that was just hilarious. The three of them sat there at the kitchen table, our own Trevi Fountain, spraying soda and juice high in the air and across the room and hooting with laughter.

That's pretty much how we handled things for thirty years or so. Try this, then that, then something else. This method of instruction was exhausting for us kids and often seemed more than useless. Margaret appeared to stop doing things only when she felt like it. Just when we gave up trying to make her stop, she'd drop some behavior that we'd been trying to break her of for months or years. Like pouring the milk down the sink. Like spitting down the front of her shirt on purpose and wiping it up with her finger. Like turning her music up really loud at certain points on the record so that we all shouted, "Turn it down, Margaret!" Like talking to herself. Like spanking the houseguests.

Why would I miss this kind of behavior? Because it was a part of me, and because it was all I had. This was how I knew my sister—as this gigantic mass of predictably destructive behavior; irrational, unpredictable motivation; and enormous affection. Growing up around Margaret, I always felt like things were about to spin out of control, and I never quite knew how to handle whatever happened next, but I was used to it. I had a recurring dream when we were younger: I was driving in a car down a treacherous, twisting road in the dark. It was icy, and I wanted to slow down, but when I pushed the brakes, nothing happened. Then I realized I was sitting on the passenger side.

I didn't see my sister much anymore. There's the old saying, you don't know what you've got 'til its gone. It wasn't that simple. It was more like you hate Jell-O, and then they take away the Jell-O and you still don't like Jell-O, but you miss having dessert, so it turns out that Jell-O was better than no dessert at all. The loss I felt was partly just life taking its course. As an adult, I'd moved and traveled as I had the liberty and facility to do so. My sister hadn't done those things, because she couldn't. She had stayed in the same place, and we only saw each other when I returned to my childhood home.

There was another reason I'd seen her less; a couple of summers before, I had told my parents I would rather see Margaret alone when I came to visit instead of seeing her at the family lake cabin. Translation: don't invite Margaret. My sister's behavior at family gatherings had become unbearable to me. Our family's response to her behavior had become even more unbearable. As my visits grew ever briefer in adulthood, they remained violently colored with dramatic outbursts from Margaret and consequential fractionalization of the family as we failed, collectively and separately, to cope. And unlike when we were children, there was no time in between these intense sessions to enjoy the good stuff. I'd return to wherever I was living at the time completely drained. I'd get migraines on the plane, pulled muscles in my neck and back. I'd go back to work feeling exhausted, feeling like I hadn't really been on vacation. I don't know how Margaret felt, but I'd be willing to bet that she was worn out, too.

So she wasn't invited. The rest of us gathered at the cabin, and these visits were quieter and calmer than we'd ever experienced before as a family. And when I saw Margaret separately on my visits home, she was like a person transformed. I'd pick her up at her house for lunch or coffee, and she was quiet, watchful. She always seemed glad to see me. We had what you might call "normal" times together. And yet I felt, somehow, that I had lost something. We never discussed this issue as a family. But then we were never a family that was prone to discuss much. We were better at silent brooding or sudden fits of temper that went unresolved. I'm pretty sure, though, that my parents did not agree with me that things were better this way. Because that's what I kept telling myself: It was better this way, to draw boundaries, for her and for me, to try to act like the adult I wanted to be instead of the child I had been. I wanted to change the parameters of our relationship as I had with our other grown siblings, albeit in a more a mutual way.

PONDERING ALL OF this, I moved my hose to the rosebushes in the front of the yard and aimed at the roots to try to keep the water off the leaves. They'd been here when we moved in, eight bushes all in a tangle of thorns and weeds and broken shoots. I left them alone for the first year as we got settled in the house. In the spring I gave them the pruning of the century, or at least their first pruning of this century. I'd spent hours hunkered down on my hands and knees cutting back the dead wood, ripping out grass and weeds, whittling the crowded stalks down to a healthy few. I got my hair tangled in the branches and cut my arms on the thick thorns. When I'd finished, I stood back to look at what I'd done and felt a rush of panic. Although I felt I'd been careful in the choices I'd made, the plants just looked butchered to me. I wondered if they would ever come back. But I waited and prayed and watered them, and now here they were—gorgeous, exploding with healthy growth and enormous blossoms. I felt vindicated. But mostly I just felt happy that they were so alive. That was something I'd learned about the benefits of starting over, of trying again when I thought something was impossible.

MY DRIVE TO Spokane, Washington, was just under three hundred miles. That was four and a half hours of straight driving, with a coffee stop for me and a pit stop for Dizzy the dog. It was 10:00 PM before I pulled up in front of my brother Larry's house. We visited for a while, and then I headed out to sleep in my camper van with the hound. I woke up the next morning in front of Larry's house, looking out on the mild suburban landscape of the town I was born in. I was parked about a mile from the house I grew up in. Ponderosa pines swayed overhead in the weak sunshine. I climbed out the side door of the VW and moved stiffly toward the house with hopeful thoughts of coffee. A neighbor appeared to be staring at me as I shuffled up the driveway and into the house, but I was probably just imagining things. I had grown up thinking everyone was always staring at us. That's because they usually were.

My sister's disorder overshadowed every major event in my life from First Communion and eighth-grade graduation to my first day of college and my wedding. It's fair to say her autism loomed over me even at my birth. On my twenty-seventh birthday I sat across the table from my mother with a question on the tip of my tongue: *What was happening in your life when you were twenty-seven?* I wanted to know. She was that same age when I was born, her last child. I wanted to know what she had been thinking about as I floated there within the curve of her belly. *What did you think about me?* I wanted to ask. *What did you say to me when it was just the two of us alone?* But I never got the chance to ask. My mother was deep in conversation with my friend as we waited for our dinner to come, and I heard her say, "Margaret was diagnosed with autism in fall of 1970. She was just three years old." I felt sucker punched. My mother never noticed. But to me, my story now went like this: my birthday is the anniversary of Margaret's autism.

At Larry's I waited until I was sufficiently caffeinated, and then I drove north on Washington Street, the north-south artery that divides Spokane in half. I passed through a revived downtown area, past River-front Park, the site of Expo '74. The bridge took me across the Spokane River and up the hill into the Gon-zaga University district. We went to high school near here, all of us but Margaret. Two of my siblings went to the university, and Larry finished law school in this neighborhood. Ann and Larry got married here, and I learned how to do a beer bong. Mike had narrowly avoided wrecking the car here on more than one snowy morning as we headed to school. This neighborhood had always been a kind of proving ground for our fam-ily in one way or another. Even now, I half expected to see a younger version of my brother Larry speeding down Hamilton Boulevard with Mike in the passenger seat and me in the back with Vanessa McRae.

By the time I pulled up in front of Margaret's house it was about 10:00 AM. I got halfway up the walk before the door banged open and revealed Margaret's large frame. "Hi, Eileen!" she said. Here stood my big sister, smiling and happy to see me. What a relief. She was wearing the tan hiking pants I had bought her the previous summer and a short-sleeved zip-neck top I had picked out for her. When we had gone on a hike the previous fall, she'd been dressed in linen pants and a long-sleeved shirt. Neither had held up well in the dusty heat. Today Margaret was also sporting a raspberry fleece coat that matched the shirt. Her hair had been cut recently. She looked great, and she was smiling. Thank God.

"Hi, Eileen!" she said again and embraced me. My big, soft sister. It was a quick hug, but it was a hug. Not the no-arm lean-in I'd had last fall, when she seemed less sure about wanting to go anywhere with me. That day she would barely look at me and kept muttering under her breath, making weird faces, and avoiding eye contact when we went to REI for some rainy-day shopping.

A young woman stepped out onto the porch and introduced herself. This was Alicia, the one who had urged Margaret to call me. New to the staff, Alicia was Margaret's "focus person," the staff member who was most tuned in to my sister's daily life and tried to help her do the things she wanted to do: find a job, go swimming, run errands. Alicia was smart, cute, and genuinely warm. "Margaret was so excited that you were coming this morning," she said. And later, when I asked how Margaret had been and what she had been up to, Alicia filled me in. Margaret obviously liked her very much, as she smiled and hugged Alicia good-bye before getting into the car. As I left, Alicia told me, "I just love Margaret." I wanted to believe her. I could see how my sister would love her back. I needed to believe that Margaret was living with people who really cared about her well-being, who saw her as a person, an individual.

It was hard to believe, because I'd met a lot of Alicias: kind young women and men, often students, who did this job well and eventually moved on to better-paying, easier careers. I wanted someone to stay and be there for

Margaret always, like family. But how could I expect that of a complete stranger when I couldn't do it myself? And why was I still feeling guilty that I was not there taking care of Margaret? No one had ever asked me to, and I was certainly not qualified in either temperament or training. But I had taken care of her when we were growing up, as a matter of course. I was her big little sister, but I still felt responsible for her as an adult, and I felt guilty. As much as I was trying to accept that it just wouldn't be good for either of us, the survivor's guilt was hard to put down; I'd gotten used to the feeling of carrying that guilt on my shoulder, the way our dad used to carry a case of beer down the dock to our boat.

Margaret had now galloped down the walk to the van. Dizzy wagged her tail in greeting and got a gentle pat on the nose from my sister. We both climbed into the van. "Hi, Eileen!" she said again and gave the door a mighty slam. The van rocked from side to side as I remembered, again, that Margaret closes every door as if she's the Incredible Hulk. "Hi, Margs!' I leaned across the gap between the seats to give her another hug, still struck by her physical presence. "You look so pretty," I said, "Who gave you that coat?" She looked down at it and rubbed the fleece with her finger. "Ann," she said confidently, meaning our oldest sister, which I doubted.

"You want to go for a hike?" she asked me, but it wasn't really a question. What she really meant was "I want to go for a hike." But I responded anyway. "Yes, I do," I said, and I pulled out my notebook.

We are an anxious people, we Garvins. On this day I was anxious because it is my habit, and my sister was anxious because she has autism. Or maybe it had nothing to do with her autism; it was just the family quirk that made her disorder harder to bear. Whatever the case, for both of our sakes I had made a list of everything we would do that day. Both Margaret and I have always been compulsive list makers. Margaret would fill an entire notebook when something was on her mind, lists of words like "Lake" or "Lunch" or "Mike." Ladders of words climbed up and down the lined pages. My day planner, less linear, always looked like a key piece of the plotline from the movie *Memento*. But I figured if I planned out our day and wrote everything down, we could both refer to it if either one of us started feeling nervous. I'd written "Eileen and Margaret's List" at the top. I handed the notepad to my sister and asked her to read it. She scanned the list and swept a slender finger under each item as she read it.

"Home. Store. Hike. Lunch. Shop. Home!" She ended with a flourish.

"Where are we now?"

Margaret looked out the window. "Home!"

"What's next?"

She looked at the page. "Store!"

"Right! We are going to the store to buy some snacks for the hike." And so we did.

Huckleberry's Natural Foods store was on the south side of town. I was a little nervous about this stop, because

the store was also on the way to my parents' house, and
I didn't want Margaret to think that that was where we
were going. Or to insist on stopping by and derailing my
plans for the day. But she didn't mention it as we flew up
the hill and pulled into the parking lot at Huckleberry's.
Margaret was out of the door almost before the van
stopped moving and halfway into the building when I
caught up with her. I grabbed a basket, which I asked her
to carry. Huckleberry's was crowded. Margaret charged
through the late-morning throng with purpose, as if
she'd won a timed shopping spree. This is just how she
moves. Mostly people didn't notice. Occasionally someone sensed her moving up behind and jumped out of
the way, looking startled or irritated. I kept a stupid smile
plastered to my face, as if this would somehow amelio-
rate any trouble. "Hi! We're friendly! Just a little weird!"
That's what my smile said.

Luna bars, trail mix, apples, and water. With our items
quickly gathered, Margaret banged our basket down on
the counter. The cashier quickly shifted his gaze to me,
because my sister didn't make eye contact. But he was
friendly, nonetheless. I paid. I said thank you. We left.

"What's next, Margaret?" I asked my sister.

"Hike!" she said. Now she was grinning.

INTERSTATE 90. IT'S one of the longest in the country,
stretching from Seattle to the Midwest. For thirty years
my family had used about thirty miles of it to get back and
forth from town to "the Lake," which was what we call

Lake Coeur d'Alene. The section we'd always traveled took us from downtown Spokane to open land that used to look like country: cows grazing, the occasional horse, homey old farmhouses under the shade of tall willows. Any semblance of country between Spokane and Lake Coeur d'Alene had disappeared during the 1990s. First came the outlet malls, and then housing developments sprang up on the shoulders of hills like acne on a teenager. The traffic was now constant and thick. I wondered where all these people were going and where you might work if you lived out here.

When I was a kid, the open space out here would lull me into a doze by the time we reached our marina. It was a beautiful transition time, taking us from our busy lives in town to the quiet tempo of lake life. All seven of us would pile into a Chevy van with cats and dogs and the birds in a birdcage and food for a week or more at a time. We'd drive to the marina, load the boat, and speed across the short stretch of water between the dock and our place, unload the boat, and then there we were. Our own line of sandy beach, our splinter-inducing dock, deep cool water, and the quiet woods behind the house. Since 1973 this had been our gathering place, this secluded spot with no road. Anyone who came had to arrive by boat and stay after dark. A paradise or a prison, depending on your take. Often for me that depended on what kind of mood my sister was in and what kind of reaction her actions incited in the rest of the family

As I mentioned, we'd had some wonderful times at the

cabin without Margaret in the past couple of seasons. My father wrote me an e-mail after the first experiment saying he'd never had a better time. He didn't mention the fact that my sister was not there. But the rest of us siblings had felt more relaxed because we weren't hold- ing our collective breath all weekend. Maybe my dad felt that, too. As for my sister Margaret, I truly believed that being out there with all of us had made her unhappy. Not when we were children, but when we were young adults. She never made it through a visit without completely melting down. And when she wasn't upset, she was with- drawn, listening to her music and rocking, trying to build a wall against the rest of us. On a normal Saturday in July there might be twenty people in the place, all talking and laughing, playing music. How could this have been fun for Margaret? How could she not have a blowup? When I thought of it that way, it made sense to me that my sister was so calm, so quiet when I spent time alone with her. And I could believe, during these hours, that this was a good time, a period of transition into some- thing new and better for all of us.

MARGARET AND I rode along and felt the road move under the tires. Neither one of us said much. But it was an easy silence. Easier, anyway, than it had been in the past. As we neared the exit for the town of Coeur d'Alene, I got nervous. We would pass our marina on the way to the hike I'd chosen. Even though she said she wanted to go hiking, this could be disastrous, since disrupting

Margaret's routine has always been a sure way of setting her off. I was picturing myself driving east on I-90 with my sister wailing and thrashing in the passenger seat as I tried to keep the van on the road: "You're going to the LAAAAAAKE! You're going to the LAAAAAAKE! Aaaaaaaaah!" over and over again. That's what I saw in my head. That's what I used to see all the time. My sister. Freaking out and inconsolable. (And a driving hazard, I might add.) But I was wrong again. We passed right by the exit to our marina, and Margaret simply turned her head to watch it go past.

Ten more miles of I-90. Three miles of Highway 97 south. We pulled into the trailhead and climbed out of the car. I had brought my CamelBak for Margaret to wear and loaded another pack with water, snacks, sunscreen, and a map. My intention was to make sure Margaret, a novice hiker, was as comfortable as possible so that she'd have a good time. Boy, did I feel prepared. I managed to get the CamelBak straps over Margaret's slender shoulders, but the waist strap just wouldn't meet in her Rubenesque middle. So the CamelBak was going to have to hang from her shoulders. She seemed okay with that.

"Ready?"

"You're going hiking, Eileen!"

I couldn't believe how smoothly things were going. What had I been worried about back there in my front yard?

"Let's go!" I said to Margaret, and to Dizzy, who leaped in the air and licked my nose. I turned my heel and headed toward the trailhead. We were off to see the freaking wizard!

Then behind me I heard Margaret say, "Lunch?"

My heart sank. I knew I'd forgotten something.

"Margaret, what did you have for breakfast?"

"Froot Loops!"

Terrific. Not exactly the breakfast of champions. And that had probably been about five hours ago, since she usually rose at dawn. So I handed my sister a peanut butter Luna bar and hoped for the best.

It was a climb. The trail moved up through tall shadows of Ponderosa pine. Snowberry and thimbleberry bushes bordered the soft track of dirt and needles. Wild lupine, yarrow, and daisies splashed the green with color. Dizzy bounded up the trail and into the bushes and circled back to us over and over again, smiling her enigmatic canine smile.

My sister broke a sweat within the first few minutes. She wasn't huffing and puffing, but she was breathing hard. I slowed down. We took a break in the shade. I showed her how to use the CamelBak to suck out the water. We are both healthy perspirers, and Margaret's underarms were already soaked. So were the straps of my CamelBak. I had not foreseen this element in sharing gear until now. I didn't know what disturbed me more: the fact that my big sister was sweating all over my pack or the fact that she was wearing a pack that I had sweated all over. I tried to think about the Shasta daisies to get my mind off the bacteria.

We climbed. We rested. We drank water. There was no one else on the trail. It was absolutely quiet but for the sound of our feet, the jingle of Dizzy's collar. Every once in a while we heard a voice float up from the lake below, the peep of a chickadee, the musical call of a flicker. As the crow flies, we were only a few miles from our childhood lake cabin, and yet we'd never been on this trailhead before. The smell of the woods and the water was familiar, built into my memory of summer and childhood. I imagined it was familiar to Margaret, too.

WE BOTH WANDERED freely in those woods when we were children, me with a pack of brothers and cousins. Margaret was more apt to wander off by herself. When we were very young, my mother had clipped a rope to the back of Margaret's life jacket to make sure she didn't head off by herself. But it didn't take her long to figure out how to take it off if she wanted to. She was quick, smart. Margaret the Fox, my parents called her. She'd get focused on something and wouldn't seem to hear people calling her. She went missing more than once, which was terrifying to me because of the look it put on my mother's face. Her absence would put the household in an uproar. I never forgot the sound of fear in my mother's voice as we hiked the hill behind the house calling my sister's name.

But just as she always stopped hitting and spitting and pinching when she felt like it, Margaret always showed up eventually, usually before dark. Years later we discovered that she had befriended the Ulmans, the cookie-making couple down the bay. That must have been where she was much of the time. Margaret and the Ulmans had first met in their kitchen one day after she had let herself into their house to make toast. Margaret didn't speak much then, so she would have been unable to explain herself. Apparently they welcomed her just the same, let her make herself toast, sit and eat it, and leave silently. She came back later to make cookies. Another one of her secrets.

HIKING, WE MADE it about halfway into the 3.5-mile loop, which is to say that if we turned around there, we would end up covering the same distance as if we'd completed the loop, but without the satisfaction of going full circle. But by the time we reached this place in time and caloric output, there was no convincing Margaret that up is the same as down. She had had enough.

"Lunch?" she asked. "You're gonna have lunch, Eileen?"

The problem with lunch was that it was fifteen miles back in the other direction. Hindsight told me I should have turned around at the trailhead, eaten lunch, and come back this way before attempting to hike. But I didn't. So there we were.

"After the hike, Margs."

We walked on in silence.

"You're gonna have lunch, Eileen." This no longer sounded like a question.

"How about a snack, Margs?" I dug in my pack and

handed her another Luna bar. She looked down at it, and then she looked at me. The Luna bar bounced off my forehead and landed in the bushes.

"You don't want the Luna bar, Margs?" Like I was just guessing.

"No! You don't want the Luna bar. Lu-NA bar! Lu-NA-bar!"

Now she was pissed. She let fly with a string of nonsense words and extraterrestrial noises that were so familiar to me. She kicked her legs against the trail and flung one arm high in the air, ending with an angry "WHHH-HOOA!" I was still in denial.

"How about some trail mix?"

She grabbed the bag from me. I could tell she was hungry in that urgent way that you get hungry when you're out of shape and asking your body to do something it's not prepared for. She started shoving chocolate drops in her mouth. I knew I shouldn't be, but I was annoyed. "Margaret, eat some raisins and nuts, too."

She complied, but avoided the other dried fruit or chucked it onto the trail, where Dizzy happily chased after it. Margaret was breathing hard and not smiling anymore. It was clear to me that our hike was over. I surrendered.

"Do you want to go to lunch, Margs?" I asked.

"Yes!" Her face lit up, and she jumped to her feet and started walking down the trail, abandoning the trail mix, her CamelBak, and me.

My sister was not much for transitions. On or off.

Going or staying. Clothed or suddenly quite naked. These things happened fast. In her mind, we should have been back in the car already. Hurrying so that I wouldn't lose sight of her, I packed up everything she had left behind, stuffed it into my pack, and started down the trail behind her.

Dizzy was joyful, sensing the turnaround, and bounded along behind Margaret. I was disappointed and trying not to be. I mean, who really cared if we finished the loop? Would that have meant the hike was "successful"? Would that have meant Margaret had a good time, that I was, by that measure, a "good sister?" Was she even aware of my being here? Was she just somewhere else in her head? How was I supposed to even begin to connect with her if we couldn't talk or sustain some kind of mutual activity anyway? This was probably just my own low blood sugar talking, but I was discouraged. No, *discouraged* doesn't capture it. I was being a sore loser, a poor sport. I wasn't getting my way, and I was pissed. I still seemed to be hung up on some expectation I'd had about how great everything would be for me, for Margaret, if I just tried a little harder to make things work. We headed down the hill, and I moved out in front, grumbling to myself. What I didn't ask myself outright but was working toward was, Why bother? Why did I even make the trip? Six hundred miles round-trip for what? What kind of relationship could I honestly expect to have with my sister, and why shouldn't I just throw in the towel? If she didn't care, why the hell should I waste any more time than I already had?

I heard my sister stop on the path behind me. I turned around and looked at her. She glanced over her shoulder, then back at me.

"Dizzy," she said, and pointed into the brush.

My dog, who had been off her leash, was nowhere to be seen. She'd disappeared off the trail into the bushes, chasing a chipmunk, perhaps, or, more likely, a phantom crust of sandwich. Margaret turned around now and was gazing into the wall of green surrounding us, silent and waiting. It dawned on me that she was waiting for Dizzy. She was worried about my little dog, or something like worried, and wanted to make sure Dizzy wouldn't be left behind. She understood that we three were together. This went straight to my heart.

"Dizzy!" I called.

"Dizzy!" Margaret called. "Dizzy! Where's Dizzy?" She was not using her pissed-off alien voice, but her regular voice.

"Dizzy! Here Diz!"

"Where's Dizzy?"

"Dizzy, come! Dizzy!"

Soon, we heard the beat of small paws, and Dizzy's head emerged from a thicket of thimbleberries with great verve. "Ta-da!" she seemed to be saying. "Here I am!"

"There's Dizzy!" I said.

"There she is!" my sister said. "There's Dizzy!" She gave Dizzy a pat as my dog leaped back onto the trail and bounded past us. We continued on in a happy silence punctuated by the sound of our eight feet. We reached the bottom of the trail and headed to the van. As we crossed the parking lot, I reached into my bag and took Dizzy's leash out of my pack. Wordlessly, Margaret took it out of my hand, bent down, and clipped it onto Dizzy's collar as if it were something she did every day, and led my dancing little dog toward the van. A trio once more, our hearts were lighter: Margaret's because we were getting ever closer to lunch, Dizzy's because she'd found some delectable and unmentionable snack in the brush, and me because it always made me feel happy when someone loved my dog. That much my sister could give me.

LUNCH WAS EASY. We ate at a favorite family burger joint in Coeur d'Alene, happily getting a place at the counter after a brief wait. We hunched over our burgers in a companionable silence. The place was full of regulars, the air steamy with the scent of grilling meat. Nobody was talking much, as they were too focused on eating what was in front of them and trying to decide if they should give up their barstool or order another greasy delight. A few tourists wandered in and started wondering aloud if it was worth the wait and why they didn't serve French fries here. Everybody at the counter, except for Margaret, rolled their eyes and kept chewing.

Later, we stood on the sidewalk outside the diner. "What's next, Margaret?" We consulted our list.

"Shop!" she read.

"Okay, shop it is."

I didn't know why I had put shopping on the list, except that it seemed like a normal activity, something to extend our visit together. We walked down Sherman Avenue, a street that had become busier every year. Herds of tourist families waddled past, sucking on waffle ice cream cones, or stood in the middle of the crosswalk arguing about where to go next, oblivious to the idling traffic waiting for them to proceed. It seemed like every block had a couple of new restaurants, rock 'n' roll blaring out onto the patio, young people drinking beer and shrieking with laughter. Margaret and I were both unnerved. We both have trouble with noise, although Margaret, having autism, is usually the more intolerant one. After all, I am supposed to be the normal one.

We took a left and moved down a quieter street. Some parts of the town looked exactly the same as they had when we first started coming here in 1973. Like us, some things had remained the same as others changed. *Change isn't always good or bad,* I thought. It's finding the balance that matters, and remembering to appreciate where you are when you're there.

Margaret hadn't looked at me since we'd left the burger joint. "Shop!" I heard her say under her breath. "You're going shopping! Shopping!" As if she were saying,

"Ah, shit!" Who was I kidding? I'd always hated shopping almost as much as she did.

"What do you think, Margaret? Do you want to go home?"

And suddenly her face was awash in sunshine. "Yes, please, Eileen!"

Back at the van, we climbed in and headed west into a light rain. Neither of us said a word all the way home. We were full. We were tired. It was enough. As I dropped Margaret off at her house, I felt happy that I'd made the trip. It didn't matter that we hadn't finished the hike. It didn't matter that we hadn't gone shopping, like normal sisters. I was no longer mad that on the way to lunch Margaret had reached over and shoved me, as I knew she would, just as I headed into a curve on the highway going about eighty miles an hour. That she immediately threw her arms around my neck in apology didn't help much, being nearly as dangerous as the shove, but I'd managed to keep the van on the road.

What did matter was that we'd both done our best to spend the afternoon together. That made me feel happy, and I was pretty sure it made Margaret happy, too. She grinned and waved energetically at me as I stood on her porch saying good-bye. "Okay! Thanks for the lunch! Thank you very much for coming, Eileen! G'bye, Dizzy!" And still waving and grinning madly, she slammed the door in my face.

MONTHS PASSED. The summer had flown by and I hadn't gone to visit again. I'd spoken to Margaret, briefly, over the phone. I'd made plans with one of her staff members to bring her down to my house for a visit. This would take some doing. Logistically, it called for a two-and-a-half-hour drive on my part to meet Margaret and Clifford, who had volunteered to drive her halfway in his own car. Then we would head to my house for the afternoon, evening, and the next day and night. The day after that, we would head back to the same meeting place after lunch, where I would drop her off. In my head this all sounded great. I had activities planned that I hoped would please us both. But I was also back to the not knowing, the uncertainty of the future. This was an experiment, and I had no way of knowing what would really happen once she got here or how either of us would feel until we were living through it together.

I WAS OUT in the yard again at the beginning of fall. The sun and water of a gorgeous summer had turned the backyard into a jungle. High over my head, the fennel waved its fragrant plumes in the air. The yarrow had spread itself the length of the beds. Lemon balm rose, leggy and dry, up past my waist. Sunflowers loomed well over seven feet, their heavy heads nodding in the afternoon wind. I knew what I needed to do without anyone telling me, and yet it seemed impossible—impossible, that is, until I began. For hours I cut and cleared, removing any leaf or stalk that seemed to have spent itself. My piles turned into mounds and filled the back of the pickup truck.

When it was over, I knew I had done the right thing.

The plants that were still standing seemed to be stretching themselves out, taking in the sun and the air. The pruning made the yard seem more open, sparer. There was a beauty in the spaces between things. But there were a few spots, here and there, that simply looked empty. Beds, for example, where I dug out hundreds of iris rhizomes because they took too much water, created too much mess, sapped my energy. Those spots seemed like holes, gaping and wanting. I didn't yet know what would go there, what would happen next. Something good, I was sure, would happen in those spaces. Some beautiful plants would eventually take the place of that emptiness and would teach me something else I never knew about color and fragrance and growth. I would just have to wait and see what happened. After all, there was no rush.

Like my life, this was just another season.

10.

life is a bowl of spaghetti

There are gentle ways to acclimate your visitor to the way things are in your household and help her fit right in without causing annoyance or conflict on either side. . . . This in no way means that you can insist that she do everything your way—after all, she is your guest and her happiness and comfort are important, too.

—*On House Guests,* EMILY POST'S ETIQUETTE

ARGARET WAS SCREAMING, and the whole world stopped. We were trapped, all of us, inside the sound of her voice, a piercing, anguished wailing that felt like it would never stop. Somehow I couldn't remember the sound of the world before, when it had been quiet and calm, when we had all been walking down the street together just talking, the five of us. Before we got in the car. Before Margaret had started screaming.

My mother was in the driver's seat, sitting across from Margaret. Mom was speaking, but I couldn't hear the sound of her voice or make out what she was trying to say. Her face looked calm from where I was jammed between Brendan and his best friend, Rob, in the back-seat of my mother's ancient Mercedes. We were on our way to dinner. We *had* been on our way to dinner. And then Margaret couldn't find the case to the tape she had been listening to all day—Ravel's *Bolero*. Then the world tilted, and we were all trapped by the panicked loss of a piece of plastic.

Before the screaming started, I had been experiencing a family visit. I can't say "enjoying," because that isn't really accurate. This was the mid-90s, and my mother had driven herself and my sister across Washington State to come stay with me in Seattle. *Bolero* was blaring out of the speakers when they pulled up to the curb outside my apartment on Capitol Hill. The car was still moving when Margaret threw open the car door to greet me, and the crescendo of Ravel's march came with her. It was like a parade. "Hi, Eileen! You're going to see the Space Needle!" Margaret said. Without having to ask, I figured they had probably listened to *Bolero* over and over again during the three-hundred-mile drive—through the desert, across the Columbia River, up into the mountains, over the pass, and down into Puget Sound. And I knew then that *Bolero* would be our soundtrack for the week. This was my sister's way. She'd choose a theme song—or, if we were luckier, a whole theme record—which she would compulsively play again and again for a period that might last days, or, in some cases, years.

I stood on the curb feeling depressed as I watched my sister climb out of the car. I knew Margaret had been looking forward to this visit. With her severe autism, my sister does not have a long list of hobbies. It was difficult for us to find activities to share with each other. But car travel she loved. The elevator in the Space Needle, ditto. The Seattle Aquarium, the monorail, seeing me—it all seemed like a perfect combination, for her at least. But even with her excitement on the first day, I knew from experience what a challenge she could be as a guest. I knew what kinds of things could happen. As they eventually did: The case to the *Bolero* tape had gone missing, and she had just lost her shit.

We were all locked into the car. Even if the door locks hadn't been automatic, none of us would have been able to move anyway. The force of my sister's rage had rendered everyone immobile as we watched her sound off. Margaret screamed with her whole body, her entire, powerful 180-pound body. Her torso was the instrument of her rage. Her mouth was open wide, and the scream went on and on in between breaths. She arched her back and launched herself against the back of her seat, slamming herself against it so hard that I thought she might join us in the backseat. Eyes closed, she kicked her feet, grabbed the sun visor, the glove box, anything she could put her hands on. Her cry, which had started as a question, had become a howl of despair. It was like being in a tornado. We were all just sitting there, packed into the car like pickles in a mason jar, watching. Even though I couldn't hear her, I knew my mother was trying to reason with Margaret, but I doubted my sister could hear anything at all. The old sedan rocked from side to side with the force of my sister's rage. Brendan and Rob looked terrified, and I couldn't quite believe that the police hadn't arrived yet.

Why did she need the tape case? I would never know the answer to that. But the loss had set off an uncontrollable, raging panic. I had lived with her for eighteen years, shared a bedroom, a bathroom, hundreds of holidays and special occasions. My parents had lived with her for twenty-one years. Nobody had figured it out. What were we supposed to do? Why was she doing it? When would she stop? What should we do next time? We couldn't actually ask these questions when we were in the thick of it, because the screaming was all we could think about. It was like being caught in an avalanche: You can't recall what you learned in snow safety class, because you are too busy fighting to stay alive. Even by the time I had moved to Oregon, I hadn't found the answers to these questions. But I could say this much: It was quite something to be in the same situation time and time again and never find the way to deal with it, never feel like what I was doing was the right thing to do. This continued failure weighed on me.

Objects had always anchored my sister. The chair went *here*. The hardback copy of *Heidi* went on the table at an angle. The Ella Fitzgerald *Porgy and Bess* record was always in precisely *this* spot. And the winter boots were in the front closet in a row. The Ravel tape case was important for some unexplainable reason. But that reason, unknowable to the rest of us, kept the car from sliding off the road, kept the sky from falling, and kept the sea off the shore. Without it, there was no hope. That much I could see from where I was sitting.

Finally, after what seemed like hours, I unfroze and unlocked my door, opening it into the other world outside the car. I felt the rush of cool, salty air from Puget Sound, and we all suddenly remembered to breathe. Rob, Brendan, and I started hunting for the tape case. We searched the backseat and floor several times, with no luck. "But it's a car, for Christ's sake, not a football field," I said. "It's got to be in here somewhere." Then suddenly Rob plucked it off the floor with two fingers and held it up in front of him, marveling at it like it had fallen from the sky. Margaret snatched it from his fingers, and the screaming stopped like a turned-off faucet. "It was just lying down there," Rob said with wonder in the quiet car.

We all breathed in and then out, and then in again. Our hearts slowed their racing. It had begun to rain, and I shut the car door and cracked the window. We sat there for a moment, all of us quiet, and the sound of the rain on the roof was clear and beautiful. Margaret popped in the tape, and Ravel's *Bolero* began its tentative way, the delicate melody dancing its way into our hearts. We put on our seat belts, and nobody said anything for a long time.

After a while Margaret, still half sobbing, exclaimed, "There he is! There's the tape case, Mom! There's

Bolero!" She was so joyful. "Okay! That's good manners, Mom!"

We all laughed a little hysterically and agreed with her. Then my mother drove us to dinner at a restaurant on Lake Union, where everybody, except for Margaret, had way too much to drink.

SUCH WAS A typical visit from my big sister. And the *Bolero* incident, I remembered, had happened early in the trip. Things hadn't gotten any easier after that. The visit included more panic, more screaming, more failure, and my growing anger. Those were the years before I had learned how to treat Margaret's outbursts like the weather, to be like a passerby caught in a storm: get inside out of it. Sit and watch from a safe place. Do what you can to help the person caught in it, but don't get too close, or you'll get dragged into the raging river.

That visit had happened years ago, but the tracks were still fresh. *So what the hell was I thinking,* I asked myself, *by inviting my big sister to come visit me for a couple of days in Oregon?* Even as I hung up the phone after talking with Clifford, her caregiver at the group home, I wondered if I was crazy. The plan was to have her down for three days and two nights, just the two of us. Like normal sisters.

"I've told Margaret the plan, and she is very excited about it," Clifford told me. I'd met him several times. He was a tall, friendly man in his forties who made his living by helping care for my big sister and her three housemates. He'd told me that he thought it would be really good for Margaret to take this trip. His enthusiasm made me feel worse. Shouldn't I, the family member, have been more excited? I mean, this was, after all, my idea. What did I think I was going to gain, realistically, by inviting my sister to come visit? And if I didn't know, why had I suggested it in the first place?

Brendan had asked me the same question, in a different way, the first and last time Margaret had visited me in Hood River, when she'd breezed through with her housemate and two staff members on the way home from the coast the summer before. "What did you expect, Eileen?" Brendan had asked, not unkindly, as I recounted events, weeping. "Pretty much what happened," I said, laughing. He smiled at me and shrugged, but when I came up with this harebrained idea, I had his full support—theoretically, that is. During the actual visit, he would be out of town.

The week before Margaret's visit, I got organized. I caught up on work, cleaned the house, and planned our activities. I also made sure I had food in the house that I knew she would eat; that meant several boxes of macaroni and cheese, spaghetti, and Cheerios. I was nervous. I was making lists of things she might like to do. I told myself not to have grand expectations, to just accept what came. But underneath all this optimism was the current of the past pulling me back into the way things had always been, a hole in the river that threatened to suck me under and keep me in a place of uncomfortable sameness. As much as I wanted to move forward, to create a new frame of reference for us as sisters, as a family, I feared that we would remain stuck in the eddy that had held us for so long.

As I drove to the store to pick up the Margaret-specific items on my list, I reminded myself that people could change. Our visit could actually be different from the days of *Bolero*, the years I had lived in Seattle. *For starters,* I thought, *this visit was my idea.* That hadn't been the case before.

DURING THE SEATTLE years, Margaret's visits were my mother's idea. Margaret was living in a group home and had a part-time job at a workshop for people with disabilities. My mother thought it fitting that she take a vacation just like everyone else. Somehow or other, I became the Vacation. Over the course of a few years when I was in my mid-twenties, it became an annual pilgrimage of sorts. "You're going to Seattle to see Eileen; you're going to visit the Space Needle," was how my sister put it.

On some level, of course, I welcomed these visits. They were coming all that way to see me, right? And this was family. Here I was, blindly groping my way through the mysterious rules of our unique family code, bumping up against the acceptable and the unacceptable, all unspoken. I often found myself at odds with what was expected of me and what I really wanted. I did my best to act like the good daughter and kind sister. But every time Margaret and Mom appeared on my doorstep and my sister, ignoring my greeting, shoved her way past me and sprinted into my apartment building with her suit-case, signaling the start of the Vacation, I felt like run-ning in the other direction.

For one thing, my studio apartment on Boren Avenue wasn't exactly built for three. To make room, I slept on the floor and gave them my Murphy bed. It was a slum-ber party! Just us girls! But one of us girls kept getting stepped on in the middle of the night by people trun-dling to and from the bathroom. And that same girl was sleeping on the floor. The floor! Plus, I had become accustomed to my quiet little studio and the delightful privacy that followed nearly two decades of sharing a bathroom with six other people. So I lay awake at night listening to Margaret whisper or snore, feeling invaded, too cowardly to speak up. Why didn't I ask them to get a hotel room? Because in an Irish Catholic family, asking someone to spend a little money to make life more con-venient for you is practically a cardinal sin. So I didn't say anything. I just became surlier as the week wore on and my sleep deprivation increased. But my mom didn't say anything. This was the kind of passive-aggressive response my people embraced as normal.

I almost welcomed the early mornings of these visits, because they put an end to my exhausting attempts at trying to sleep. While my guests slept in, I'd get up off the floor, put the cushions back on the couch, shower, and walk downtown to work at the small publishing com-pany where I was the only employee. My boss, a likable, anxious man, always made me a latte from his personal espresso machine during our mid-morning break. As he waited for the shots to drip, he would pull his hair out from the sides of his head with both hands and wonder aloud how in the world we were going to manage to stay afloat for another month. He'd tell me how hard it was to be a small-business owner, always teetering on the brink of disaster. I'd accept my latte, feeling like I might cry, and then I'd wander back to my desk believing I was supposed to save the company. Hours would pass, and then I'd hike back up the hill to entertain my houseguests.

Anxiety had always been a prominent feature of our family culture, a common interest, you might say, but in Margaret it played a starring role. Keeping a certain maniacal sameness in her life calmed her. And unless you were a complete idiot, you'd see that the order kept her happy, so you'd better damn well stick to the program, too. When she was at home, Margaret's schedule was like clockwork: mealtimes, showering, work hours, bedtime. She rivaled the U.S. Marines for order. It was like boot camp, only she was the troops and the drill sergeant all rolled into one. I imagined that her routine had become even more rigid since she had moved into her group home and no longer had the rest of us screwing things up for her.

Whatever the case, visiting Seattle disturbed her careful routine. Even though she wanted to make the trip, all the change and upheaval was difficult for her to cope with. So, in an attempt to fend off the anxiety created by the change, Margaret created a program for the Vacation. She divided her day into two parts—Before Eileen Gets Home and When Eileen Gets Home. She'd enjoy the day sightseeing with my mother, but all the while they'd be talking about what we were going to do When Eileen Gets Home. At the Space Needle, on the monorail, at Pike Place Market—the conversation was the same.

"Mom? You're going to go out to dinner?"

"When Eileen gets home, we are going to go out to dinner, Margaret."

"When Eileen gets home, you are going to go out to dinner, Mom."

"That's right, Margaret."

"You're going to change your clothes?"

"When Eileen gets home, you are going to change your clothes, Margs."

"When Eileen gets home, you are going to change your clothes, Mom."

"That's right, Margaret."

"Mom? Mom. Mom, you're going to go back to the apartment, Mom?"

"Yes, Margs. When Eileen gets home, we are going to go back to the apartment."

"When Eileen gets home, you are going to go back to the apartment, Mom."

So it went for eight hours. Unfortunately for me, Margaret didn't think of this time as After Eileen Gets Home. "After" could have designated an ambiguous stretch of time, aimless hours moving into the evening during which we could do any or all of the things they had discussed. My sister said "when" all day, so as soon as she caught sight of me climbing up to Boren Avenue, she was ready to hustle. There was no "Hi-honey-how-was-your-day?" Margaret would have liked to grab me by the arm and shove me into the car so that we could hurry off to the next activity, whatever it might be. The specifics didn't matter. We just had to get on with the agenda for When Eileen Gets Home to feed the hungry beast of her anxiety.

I was usually hot and irritable after climbing up the hill from Pioneer Square. My childhood fear of the bus made me choose the walk instead of enjoying the convenience of public transportation. My journey home took me through Occidental Park, a crowded twenty-four-hour party of junkies and drunks who hollered at me and everybody else walking by. Sweating, tired, and worrying about how my job might disappear overnight, I rounded the corner to my street and found my edgy sister waiting for me on the front steps of my apartment building. As soon as she caught sight of me, Margaret hopped up, nervously twisting her fingers together, and said, "When Eileen gets home, you're going to go out to dinner, Eileen. When Eileen gets home. When Eileen gets home, you're going to go out to dinner, Eileen."

If I were rewriting the screenplay of my life, this is where I would say something kind and helpful. The camera would zoom in on the younger, empathetic sister comforting her disabled sibling. We would share a moment as the sun set behind us and dramatic music came up. Our mother would look out the window at this scene and get tears in her eyes to see us connecting, our sisterly bond overcoming the obstacles created by the disorder of autism.

But this was my real life. Even though I'd been thinking to myself all the way home about how I needed to be patient, I said something like "JesusfuckingChrist, Margaret! Give me a minute!" and stomped into the building with my nervous sister on my heels. And there was my real-life, calm, patient parent holding open the apartment door, kindly urging me to get the lead out so that we wouldn't have a scene. "She's been waiting for you so patiently, Eileen," Mom said.

Feeling guilty, I grumbled, "Yes, Margaret. We are going to dinner. Just give me a minute." And then I swore not-so-under my breath as I made my way upstairs to change my clothes.

Part of the reason that I was so angry was that I didn't want to give in to her anxiety. I wanted her to try being okay, without the repetition. I wanted to be the person to break through her crazy-making routine and help her be normal. I wanted that romantic movielike fantasy to be true. But she followed me up the stairs and kept saying what she was saying until I gave in and repeated it back. "Yes, Margaret. You are going to go out to dinner when Eileen gets home." Pacified, she sat down on the couch and waited for me with her hands squeezed between her knees.

• • •

ONE EVENING DURING this challenging visit, I decided that When Eileen Gets Home, we should go to the Fremont neighborhood on the north side of Lake Union for dinner. Brendan and I had found this great little café, a just-discovered hot spot. The place had made a name for itself for the cheap, tasty Italian food, but also for the atmosphere, which was one part white linen napkins and two parts funky grunge bohemia. You could get a decent bottle of wine, but you could also draw on the paper tablecloth with crayons. It made all the lists that year for Seattle's Best Places.

I knew it was a gamble going there. For one thing, I knew we would have to wait. Waiting is not Margaret's strong suit. But they did serve Italian food, which is one of the few things I knew she would eat besides macaroni and cheese, so I thought it was worth a shot. Plus, I wanted my mom to see this place. I knew she would love it as much as I did, and the only way I was going to get her there was to take both of them.

Here lay the crux of the problem. During the course of my entire life, I had never had my mother's attention to myself. The closest I came was spending time with her and Margaret. And after I had moved out of the house, my mother only came to see me when she brought my sister. We could go anywhere I wanted, and my mom would even pick up the tab. But no matter where we went, Margaret was coming along and would inevitably contribute a bit of ruinous behavior to the evening that would make me wonder if I should have just stayed home alone. At the time, I was young and stubborn. I was also filled with what felt like hope, but was really denial, that this time Margaret would behave beautifully. This time we would have the kind of normal mother-daughter-sister vacation that I'd seen in the movies. I know now that this was the wrong way to look at things, but I didn't know any better. It was my best attempt at optimism, even though it never worked. So off we went to Fremont in search of a café called Bizzarro.

It was a busy night at Bizzarro. I put our name on the waiting list while my sister and mother sat outside. The café was so small that there was no lobby. We waited on a rough bench by the front door in the warm summer air, time dragging the sun lower and lower in the summer sky. I have a picture of this evening. Margaret has a huge smile on her face, and I am looking less than thrilled. I can't remember what she had done, but I can guess that she was torturing me with loud displays of something: Spanking? Hooting? Pinching? And then a hollered apology, "I'm sorry, Eileen! That's GOOD waiting!" followed by a bear hug. It was pretty easy to piss me off that week, and my irritation just seemed to increase her ebullient behavior. More than once I threatened to leave. But I really didn't want to leave. Leaving would mean going home to eat spaghetti in my studio apartment with the two of them. And I only had two chairs.

Plus, telling Margaret we were going to leave made us even more noticeable.

Me (sotto voce): "That's it, Margaret. If you can't wait quietly, we are going home."

Margaret (forte!): "No! No! No, Eileen! No! Ha ha ha! That's good behaving! You're going to eat spaghetti! That's GOOD waiting!"

On this particular night she was laughing as she yelled this, not crying, which didn't make her any quieter. But laughter was on the right side of normal, so we stayed. And we waited. And waited. After it grew dark and I could see the streetlight glinting across Margaret's teeth as she teased me, they gave us a table.

As the three of us followed the very hip host through the crowded bistro to our table, I felt like everyone was staring at us, even though they probably weren't, yet. This kind of paranoia was a family affliction. After years of being center stage during my sister's very public outbursts, I always felt like we were being watched. Feeling that we were the subject of observation added a buzz to my already tense state of being, so I ordered a carafe of wine before we even sat down. I couldn't complain about our table. After the long wait, it couldn't have been more perfect. We sat near the window with a broad view of the entire room. I took it all in: Strings of tiny white Christmas lights cast a magical glow on the crowded tables of twos and fours. A man sat hunched over the piano in the corner, laying down a thread of music under the buzz of voices. The wine came, and we had bread with olive oil and balsamic vinegar. My mother and I drank and talked as Margaret grew more

and more quiet. I felt so normal. What had I been worrying about? We looked over the menu and waited for
someone to come take our order.

Looking back, I imagine that this part of the evening,
the best part for me, was not so much fun for Margaret.
The place was crowded, it was hot, and she was sitting
with her back to a room full of strangers. The piano
player started playing something lively, and then everyone was talking loudly to be heard over the noise. But I
finally had my mother's ear, and I was excited to show
this place to her, share a bit of my newfound city life.

While Mom and I were chatting, Margaret decided
that she had to use the bathroom, something she often
does in a rather sudden way. Your average person might
think, "Hmmm. I think I have to pee. Nope, I don't . . .
Yep. Yep. I do. I have to pee. Should I go? Hmmm. Wonder where the bathroom is? Maybe I'll wait a few minutes and watch to see where someone else goes. I'll wait
until we order. I'll wait until we finish this drink. I'll wait
until I can ask someone. Oh, there's the sign. Hmmmm.
Ah, looks like someone just came out of there, so it must
be free. Well, okay, I think I'll go now." And then you'd
say "Excuse me," and push yourself away from the table,
put your napkin down, stand up, and carefully make your
way to the bathroom. Right?

I don't know what goes through Margaret's mind
when she decides that she has to use the restroom. But
it always looks like someone has just shouted "Now!" in
her head, at which point she leaps out of her chair and

launches herself through the crowd like Harrison Ford fleeing the police in *The Fugitive*. She'll make a mad dash toward a perceived direction of the restroom, sometimes knocking into chairs, other people, sometimes ending up in the kitchen or the men's room. Margaret has never been a petite person, so this kind of public sprinting tends to have consequences. My family is used to this, so usually one of us is not far behind, bowing and scraping our apologies to people she might have run into, and then we hurry to catch up with her and make sure the door is closed before she gets her pants down. I've chased her through lobbies, movie theaters, and cafés like this because I know that she unbuttons and unzips as she goes. She does not mean to be rude. She's just made up her mind, so you'd better get the hell out of the way.

Margaret sprinted for the restroom with my mother trailing behind smiling apologetically, leaving me alone at the table. Our cover was blown. I could feel it. The whole place was staring at the ladies' room door, which Margaret had just slammed on our mother's heels. All heads seemed to turn to me, the lone weirdo still at the Weirdo Table. Cover. Blown. Uncool. I told myself I didn't care. I downed my wine and watched the waitress circulate the tiny room.

This waitress was one of those eccentric Seattleites who had made the town so exotic to me when I first moved there from provincial Spokane. She must have been in her late thirties and was very pretty in a theatrical kind of way. She was wearing a sexy, 1930s-era dress with combat boots. Her lipstick was a badge that said, "I'm eccentric! Don't fuck with me!" This woman was part of the reason that the café had gained an aura of celebrity. She did not really wait on people; she just kind of emotionally abused them and then brought them food after a really, really long time. She'd stop in the middle of an order to tell a joke or sing a song. All the diners would stop talking to listen and then applaud hugely. She was no server. She was an artist! Purposely and purposefully conspicuous. She was one of many such neighborhood celebrities in Seattle when I first moved there. *If only I could be so interesting and sure of myself. Someone like her could save the publishing house,* I thought. I slugged some more wine and watched her, jealous and intimidated.

I heard the bathroom door bang again and saw Margaret wading through tables and chairs as she hurried back to our corner. It seemed like everyone was watching her as she plunked down in her chair saying, "There you go! You say excuse me, Eileen! That's good manners!" Margaret grabbed her glass, took a big slurp of her root beer, and slammed it down on the table. My mother reappeared, all aflutter about the Alice in Wonderland mural on the bathroom wall, which she'd photographed. She had also popped into the men's room to see if the mural continued in there. It did! She had pictures! She'd show me! All of this loud enough for other people to hear. I wanted to slither under the table.

At this moment, the Celebrity Server sauntered over to our table to take our order. She stood over us, one hand on a cocked hip like she could barely stand it, she was so bored by us already. I quickly told her what I wanted, and then she shifted her exasperated gaze to my sister, which Margaret failed to notice. Like many people with autism, my sister doesn't make eye contact as often as other people do. When she was in school, she and her classmates played card games to work on this simple part of social interaction that so many of us take for granted. It was rather hilarious to watch—four teenagers sitting around a table, cards fanned out in their hands, each one looking away from the rest, looking at the ceiling, the floor, the door. Every so often someone would mutter, "Gimme me alla your eights," while he was gazing down at his knees.

Eating dinner at a restaurant afforded multiple opportunities to help Margaret practice looking at people while she was talking. Ordering her dinner was one such occasion. But the server didn't ask my sister what she wanted. She just turned her cold stare from me to Margaret. Saying anything, even "Gimme alla your eights," would have been more helpful than this silence. Margaret simply didn't understand this kind of shift as a nonverbal cue, although my mother and I did. My mother prompted Margaret to say what she wanted. My sister nodded and pointed at the menu. *I mean, are you stupid?* she seemed to be saying. *We're here for the spaghetti, right? What do you mean what do I want to eat?* The whole reason we drove across town and waited outside in the dark for over an hour was because she'd been promised a plate of spaghetti, so what was with all the questions? My mother and I knew what she was thinking, but to practice normal social interaction, Mom gently urged Margaret to let the server in on our secret and let her know about the whole spaghetti thing.

To be fair, it was noisy and she was busy, but the woman completely missed the fact that Margaret wasn't making eye contact with her and didn't notice the interaction among the three of us. She was annoyed and leaned in. "What? Didn't hear that. What do you want?" Margaret, now looking at my mother, said, "You want spaghetti, please, Mom." She was beginning to sound worried. By this time the server was visibly irritated with us, and it dawned on me that she wasn't clueing in to Margaret's difference. She just thought we were pokey, stupid tourists. Exasperated, she finally extricated the rest of our order, grabbed the menus from us, and stalked off. My mother and I patted Margaret's hands and told her she'd done a good job. She let out a sigh and took a big gulp of her root beer.

When our food came, my sister ate quickly and so did I, as I often do in Margaret's company. For some reason I find it hard not to wolf down my food when my tablemate is doing so. She ate quickly at home, too, but I think the anxiety she was feeling in an unfamiliar place made her eat even faster. After a few minutes she put down her fork and sat back, looking pale. Although she'd eaten fast, she hadn't eaten much and sat with her hands in her lap, braiding and unbraiding her fingers. About now I felt the full force of the guilt and remorse for try-ing to have things my way. *We should never have come here,* I thought. The room was too loud and crowded for my sister, and the spicy pasta—trying so hard to be special—was probably upsetting her stomach.

Looking back, I recognize that there was so much more going on under the surface of this visit, the constant presence of certain truths that we never spoke aloud. I was mad at myself for not being more patient. I was so angry that Margaret had autism, that there was no cure, that she never seemed to get better, that she dominated my mother's attention, that I didn't know who I was sup-posed to be in this family or in this lifetime. I wasn't ever my mother's daughter. I was just Margaret's sister. And nothing I did could change any of that, but I was too young and stubborn to swallow this complicated and barbed truth or to just walk away from it.

About this time the Celebrity Server decided to launch into one of her solos. She paused right next to our table and began to sing a lively show tune. She stood over us brandishing her tray, trilling away, reveling in the atten-tion of the entire restaurant. She was slightly off key and didn't seem to care. Everyone stopped talking to watch her. As for me, I'd about had it with this woman and the atmosphere she was so bent in creating. The suburban girl rose up in me, feeling indignant about this big-city pretense. If you had asked me, a server was supposed to take your order and bring you your food. She was sup-posed to be worried about where your extra bread was, not wondering if she had everyone's undivided attention. I was annoyed that she had trespassed so far into our personal space and yet refused to see us, to see Margaret struggling to communicate. I wanted to say something to make a dent in all that seemed to be wrong with the world—my sister's disorder, this woman's indifference, my own anger. But as it turned out, I didn't have to say anything.

Margaret had had it. Like many people with autism, she is acutely sensitive to sound. My sister also has a perfect sense of pitch and simply can't bear to listen to music that is out of tune. So just as the server turned her face toward our table, her loud, flat voice pulling all the air out of the room, my sister put her fingers in her ears and let out the most terrific screech, right in the woman's face. It was like a train whistle, but two octaves higher. The train bore down on all of us and passed into our inner ears. For a minute the world felt unbalanced, and I thought I might pass out. Then the train passed through and everything was all right again.

I looked at the Celebrity Server, who was standing there with her mouth open, silent and staring. Then she dropped her tray to her side and scurried off to the kitchen, the door banging shut behind her. You could have heard a pin drop. The entire restaurant was staring at us in terrified silence. For once, I didn't care. They could stare all they wanted. It wouldn't change the fact that Margaret had slain the giant. Looking at their shocked faces, I was killing myself trying not to laugh, but I was also proud of my big sister for defending herself in the only way she knew how. I know it might sound mean find humor in the fear of a room full of strangers, but I knew there was nothing to be afraid of. And it helped balance out the fact that my sister is scared so much of the time. After all, we all have to live in this world together. My mother reached and out and took Margaret's hand, and we kept talking like nothing had happened. Soon my sister's face relaxed.

There was no more singing in Bizzarro that night. We three quietly finished our meal, and everyone else did, too, like they knew what was good for them. The server never came back to our table, but sent the host over to deal with us instead. Margaret ordered a bananas Foster, which she wolfed down. A few seconds later she suddenly went pale, grabbed her empty root beer mug, and vomited foamy ice cream barf up to the rim. The other diners were trying so very hard not to stare at our table that nobody noticed. I think we all knew it was time to throw in the towel at that point. And if our server hadn't been such a cow, we would have cleaned it up. My mother would probably still be there, washing dishes and apologizing. Instead, we left an enormous tip and fled. I never went back.

On the way home, Margaret was quiet in the backseat, staring out the window at the light rain that had started to fall. Seattle was swallowed up in the darkness and had turned on her lights to outline her tall and curvy silhouette. I sat in the front seat, giving my mom directions and looking out at the dark sky hanging over the Puget Sound, my heart full. When we were about halfway home, Margaret sighed and said, "That's better, Mom." Then in her very solemn voice, she said, "You don't yell in the restaurant, Mom. It's bad manners. You don't yell." And I wondered who she was talking about.

The images of that trip were captured in my mother's photographs and in my memory: Margaret and me at Volunteer Park. Margaret at the Space Needle. Margaret and me sitting on the Murphy bed at the John Winthrop Apartments. Brendan's father took us all for a boat ride in Portage Bay, and there are photos of Margaret sitting in the bow of the little boat with her arm around Honey, the big yellow dog that would one day be the ring bearer at my wedding. I've looked at the photographs so many times that they have become like woodcuts in my memory: the shapes of our bodies, the outline of the buildings and horizon like permanent marks on a canvas. These images, with sharp corners and deep grooves, have worn their mark year after year in my memory and our history.

There were more cafés, more outbursts. When I took my mother to meet my future mother-in-law, Margaret threw herself backward off Sharon's couch and rolled around on the floor with her shirt riding up over her big tummy, yelling and kicking her shoes against the brand-new carpet. During an anxious morning, she had picked a scab on her chin and bled onto the couch pillows, something I always wondered if Sharon noticed. The stain was still there when this couch was handed down to us years later. I watched her writhing around on the floor, seeing flashes of her belly and big breasts as her shirt flopped around, and thought, "This is not normal. This is not what I was hoping for when I introduced my mother to Brendan's family." But that's what I got.

On the last day of their visit, Margaret started to lose her cool at a café where we had hoped to eat breakfast with Brendan and his parents. My mother tried to calm her down by reading the menu with her, encouraging her to choose something to eat. Unfortunately, Margaret wanted Froot Loops. There was no cereal on the menu. My mother and I looked at each other across the table, depressed, unspoken partners in the minor social catastrophe that we knew was sure to follow when we told Margaret that there were no Froot Loops to be had. In the middle of this silent struggle, Brendan jumped up and ran across the street to the neighborhood market, bought a box of Froot Loops, and ran back. "*There's* the Froot Loops!" my sister crowed, grabbing the box out of his hand. We were saved again. And yet never saved. When Mom and Margaret finally left, waving and tooting the horn, I went upstairs and lay down on the floor, which now felt like the place I belonged. I had a migraine for three days.

MORE THAN TEN years had passed between the night Margaret barfed at Bizzarro and the planning of her first-ever solo trip to visit me. The image of the glassful of frothy bananas Foster was still as fresh in my mind as the night I threw a napkin over it and ran away into the happy obscurity of the city night. And yet so much had happened in our lives. We had grown, we had aged, and I hoped that I had learned.

And yet some things would never change. I knew I would never be privy to what my sister was thinking. She would likely continue to be ruled by the stress and compulsion that the disorder seems to wield. I couldn't save her from its whims, but I could stop taking them so personally. We wouldn't ever have the closeness of the fantasy sisters in my mind, the people who could talk on the phone and pick up where they had left off. We wouldn't have normal family vacations, but I wasn't sure I knew what that meant anyway. *Normal* for me had ceased to mean, "What I don't have." Normal was what I'd wanted back then. Normal meant "like other people." Normal meant "ordinary." But I'd been lucky enough to trade that desire for something much more interesting.

During my recent quest, one thing had become very clear to me: I would live with Margaret's autism for the rest of my life. One expert put it plainly: Siblings of people with disabilities have all the same hardships as parents—only for longer. As another writer put it, the impact of having a sibling with autism never ends. Parents usually die first, and we siblings are left to sort things out.

But other points remained unclear to me. What role would I take? Full-time caregiver did not seem a likely choice for me, although I'd been hung up on that phantom obligation for years. One reason it had been so easy for me to stay in New Mexico was that I thought I'd be stuck holding the bag if I took part in any way. But running away no longer seemed like an option. Home had called me back, and Margaret, difficult as she is, was part of the siren song. Middle ground, then—was that where I belonged? Could I carve out a place for Margaret in my life, and could she find room for me in hers?

My relationship with my sister was a paradox. Although we could never communicate like other people, I would get more of the genuine article than I did from most relationships, because she never hid her feelings. Whenever I saw Margaret, I knew she would remember me and would greet me in exactly the same way. She might be nervous or not, but she was always expecting me. It was pretty simple, really. She expected me to show up from time to time, and by God, I'd better be there when I said I would. She always opened the door when I drove up, even if she didn't always let me come in the house. "Hi, Eileen!" she'd say, like she had just seen me yesterday, and then she'd get in the car, slam the door, and wait for me to drive us to wherever we were bound When Eileen Gets Here.

I was fairly certain that this would happen when I went to meet her and Clifford at the appointed pickup spot. I was pretty sure my sister would enjoy the drive from her house to Richland, Washington. After that, all bets were off. We'd decided to meet for lunch at Red Robin, where Clifford and I would eat and she might not. She might be happy to see me, or she might be quiet and withdrawn. She might get upset and scream, but Red Robin is pretty noisy anyway, so if that happened, one of us would simply get up and walk outside with her. And after we had paid the bill, I could only hope that instead of getting back in the car with Clifford, she'd decide that she felt like coming with me for the Vacation.

Once she decided to put her suitcase in the car, I'd be satisfied. Unlike the rest of us, Margaret never hides her feelings. She can't. So at least I knew she wouldn't come for a visit unless she felt like it, unless she was all in. That's the thing about Margaret. She can't help but be exactly who she is, so now I knew what I was getting—the unexpected, always, but the real deal. My elevated expectations had slowly departed along with the yearning for some kind of normalcy. I no longer expected to blend in when I was with my sister, nor did I hope to blend in this or any other corner of my life. Blending in means you've been worked into the sauce, assimilated to the point of being indistinguishable. We should not hope to live undistinguished lives, but to revel in the rich bits and pieces that stand out and give us our flavor.

Ruminating on this, I finished putting away the groceries and went upstairs to put clean sheets on the bed in the guest room, because my sister was coming to visit.

11.

how to be a sister

Etiquette was never intended to be a rigid set of rules.
It is, rather, a code of behavior that is based on
consideration, kindness and unselfishness.

—*On Good Manners*, EMILY POST'S ETIQUETTE

WE ARE STANDING together, naked, our small toes curling against the cold floor of the linoleum in the bathroom. Cowboys and Indians crawl up and down the wallpaper toward the high window, shooting over each other's heads across a cactus desert. I am three and shivering. You are six and silent. I hug my arms to my chest as we stand there waiting outside the high, gleaming white sides of the bathtub. I bounce on my toes. *Cold. Cold. Cold.* You just stand there, not saying anything, arms at your sides, impassive.

Here comes Ann, in through the door. Ann the Beautiful. Our older sister is already almost nine, a celebrity in my small universe. I love her so much it hurts. Too bad she hates me. Hates both of us. For being babies, for not being able to do anything, not even turn on the goddamn bathtub faucets for ourselves. And yet it doesn't bother me that she treats me with the scorn of the oldest child, who is burdened with the rest of us four younger kids. I love her all the more for being superior.

Grumbling to herself, she wrenches the taps open and turns a quick heel, then comes stomping right back at some admonishment from our mother calling from the other room, where she is busy with the boys, to make sure the water isn't too hot for the little ones. And don't forget to turn it off. More grumbling. More stomping. The door slams and she's gone.

Steam rises and clouds the mirror behind us. I'm grateful for the warming air. I move toward the tub, clamber up. But it's a high climb for short legs, and for a moment I hang stuck, high-centered on the cold porcelain. Then I reach with one toe, tip, and I'm in. You climb right over the side. You are tall and gangly, like a monkey. I sit in the front, closest to the spigot. Wonderful hot water. I hold my hands out under the rushing stream, small palms up, a prayer of thanks. You sit in the back because I can make you. Even though you are older, you do it because I tell you to. Just like later, when I make you get out and sit on the side of the tub so that I can lie down and let my hair stream out like Ann does. When we three bathe together, she makes us get out of the water and wait shivering in the cold air so that she can stretch out in there.

Her golden hair looks like seaweed. She's a mermaid. She closes her eyes, and I think she looks like Sleeping Beauty. Then her eyes snap open. "Stop touching me!" she says, even though we aren't touching her. "Well, stop looking at me, then!"

You never want to lie down in there. At least you never say you do. You never say anything to me. Not a word.

I tell you to get back in and you do. We pass a bar of Jergens soap back and forth; we share a worn washcloth, like we always do, you and me. We are the youngest girls, two of the five kids, clumped together in this nighttime ritual as in so many other things. But this night is different from the others, because at some moment during this bath it dawns on me that something is wrong with you, that you are different from the rest of us. Because you are pretty much a big girl, like Ann. But you can't do anything, like me. You are tall enough to reach the faucets, and you are probably strong enough to turn them on, but you don't know how. Or maybe you know how, but I have never seen you try. I don't question any of this or even judge it. I simply acknowledge it. *You are different.*

The next thought follows so closely behind, right on top of the first, that it's like the same thing: *Because you are different, I'm different, too.* Somehow my small brain makes this leap and it stays with me, always. *My sister is different because she is autistic, so I am different, too.*

THEY GAVE YOU the label "autistic" when you were three years old. I was still in our mother's belly when she drove you to the University of Washington in Seattle for weeks of tests. Was that why I came early, trying to claim what I could of our crowded childhood? Soon you were in intensive speech therapy, ferried to and from Eastern Washington University by our mother five days a week for two years. I waited at home for both of you with our grandmother.

What else do I remember about this time? Not much. The smell of soap on our grandmother's neck when she held me, coffee on her breath. The diaper pins she wore like a badge on her sweatshirt over her heart. Later, when we are older, she tells me I would try to draw you in, saying, "Come on, honey." I'd take your hand and bring you into whatever game the rest of us were playing. But mostly I can't untangle you from the whole unit that we were before we were in school. We were all together, we five. You only stood out from the rest of us when you screamed and screamed and wouldn't stop. Or when you wandered off on your own and had to be looked for. The panic in our mother's voice when she called your name into the big, dark woods or down an empty, darkening street made me afraid.

But then we started school and the secret was out. You were my weird big sister. My first and last childhood birthday party was a painful lesson in how others would see you. The girls from my second-grade class trooped into our kitchen for the party, which consisted of a homemade cake prepared by Mom and streamers and balloons tied to the light hanging over the table. Mom hadn't planned any games like the other mothers always did. Perhaps she didn't think of it or didn't have the time. Whatever the case, there was nothing to distract my classmates from you—sitting at the table all by yourself, staring at nothing. Most of them didn't know you, because you went to a special education class at a public school. The rest of us went to the Catholic school down the street, and my classmates had seen our brothers and Ann. But here you were, the big birthday surprise.

You didn't look up at any of them as Mom urged them to sit down. Nobody moved. I was used to your staring silence, but the looks on their faces shocked me. They were afraid of you. No one wanted to sit next to you. Not even tall, awkward Daria, who'd always earned a certain tenderness from me because she reminded me of you.

I felt a burning in my chest. A mixture of shame, anger, and guilt. I fled the kitchen and started trying to organize a last-minute treasure hunt. I had to make my party better so that they would stop looking at you like that. In our dark and cluttered basement, I collected a pile of small toys, thinking I could hide them around the house and then put a list of clues together while everyone ate cake. I could do it if I hurried. Tiffany Greco had had a treasure hunt like that at her party the previous month. It was all I could think of. But then Mike saw what I was doing, and we got into a fight over a Big Bird finger puppet, his favorite. He kicked me in the stomach, and I spent the rest of the afternoon locked in the bathroom.

Did you notice any of this? Were you glad when

everyone went home so you could go back to your records? Was it upsetting to you to have so many strangers in your house?

At school that year we learned about Lourdes Cathedral in France. The holy water there was said to work miracles, cure afflictions. The blind could see, the lame could walk. It was a miracle blessing from Jesus's mother, Mary. I started saving my money, thinking that if I could go there and bring some water back, you could be healed.

Our grandmother's smile was sad when she told me it wouldn't work. "Keep praying for your sister instead," she said. Bottled magic seemed like a much better idea, but I didn't make it to France for twenty years. I prayed every night that you would wake up one day and be normal. Ta-da! "I was just kidding around," you'd say.

Grade school was a time of plaid. Four of us marched through the seasons in our Catholic school uniforms and knee socks, our red cardigans stiff at the cuff from nose wiping. The year was a cycle of feast days, report cards, Christmas break. You wore regular clothes and took the short yellow bus from the corner. Mom waited with you every morning, holding your hand until the bus came and you climbed those stairs.

When I went to your classroom, it looked like so much more fun than mine—little tables and chairs instead of desks, colorful toys. One of your classmates, an older boy, picked me up and held me in the air, laughing. He seemed like a giant, and when he returned me to earth,

I stood looking up at his laughing face. There was playground equipment at your school. The smell of the dark wood and the feel of the coarse monkey bars under my hands made me envious. We had tetherball, four square, kick ball, that was it. It never occurred to me that you couldn't run out there and play every day at recess like I would have.

In 1975 we both got what our pediatrician said was Yersinia, or bubonic plague, along with hundreds of other children in our town. My crowded hospital room was just across the hall from yours, but I felt homesick for you, because I couldn't see you. I woke to find you sitting on the floor next to my bed, knees pulled up under your nightgown and your ankles crossed, staring at the floor. Did you come to find me? Later when I woke up, you were gone. I was so lonely, but the mean nurse wouldn't come, and I pooped my pants. The nice nurse came later and cleaned me up, but I just wanted to be at home with you and Ann in our crowded, messy room.

SUMMER WAS A bright stretch in our year, a patch of sunshine we greeted in bare feet on the wooded lakeshore. From the ceremonious opening in the spring until Labor Day, we were at the lake, and the house filled up with our laughter, traces of the beach brought in on our feet, the sound of the water at night. The days were full of our comings and goings, adventures in the woods, jumping off the cedar dock into cool sheets of water, lunch in wet bathing suits and towels, endless reading in the long afternoons, large dinners with a dozen or more people crowded around the long table.

You would blend in through all of this commotion, unless something upset you. Then your fire-engine wailing could clear the house. Lucky for us we didn't have many neighbors out there, so no one called the police.

But there was also a time that the lake house was quiet. The stillness was a kind of reprieve from the human locomotion that was the usual summer mix of friends and family. The days needed no names, because they were all long and sunny, but perhaps it was a Thursday morning, like this one. I'd wake alone in my tree-shadowed room, moved from sleep by the sound of a boat puttering by, the furious chatter of a squirrel in the woods behind the house, or the gentle silence of the house empty of motion. I'd lie in my large hundred-year-old bed, breathing an ancient, pleasant mildew, watching the sunshine dapple the painted wood walls and catch the vibrant colors of the tattered wool Oriental rug. Like everything else left in this house by the previous owners, the hand-painted china, the furniture and art, it had once been grand, but was now worn by time and our rough-playing family of seven. We were living our present among the tattered remnants of someone else's past.

I'd get up in my bare feet and nightgown in my room at the head of the hallway, the other doors along the hall standing closed. I might hear our father snoring in the master bedroom at the other end. I was so quiet passing your room. I could see you there, not moving, so still. It was a miracle. As soon as you woke up, you were all noise and motion. Running feet, slamming doors, snapping on the stereo, and launching one album after another, all day, until darkness fell and they made you go to bed. Roger Whittaker. *Victory at Sea.* The Osmonds. Those were the good days.

On the bad days there was your screaming, your inconsolable anger and fear. The house was electric with collective anxiety, and there was nothing I could do. Best to let you sleep as long as possible.

Down the turning staircase, past the French doors on the landing, into the large open room on the first floor. I'd walk out onto the sun-drenched steps; the house, facing northeast, always caught the morning sun. A soft breeze blowing inland in my face. Thursday morning. No boats, no people, no Jet Skis, which came later, no tour ferries. Me, a cat, the breeze, the lake, the birds, and you not here—sleeping in.

We have a picture of you taken in 1974, when you were seven. You had climbed up on a rock-covered barge at the end of the beach and sat high up on the seat of the tractor, your hands tucked into your life jacket. Your hair is a mess, and you've picked a scab on your face, so it is bloody. You are looking at the camera but not seeing the person holding it. That picture always made me feel so lonely. I didn't understand why you wanted to sit over there by yourself on the cold steel seat of the tractor. I didn't understand what was wrong with you. I'd never known you to be any other way, so I never questioned it.

You were a strange child, but you never seemed strange to me. You were just yourself. When our friends came to visit and saw you lying in the middle of the room on your back spinning an orange cushion in the air, it must have looked so bizarre. *Spin, spin, spin,* and then *pop!* You'd kick the cushion high, flip it over, and catch it on your slim ankles without missing a beat. You never dropped it. They'd stop and stare. "That's just Margaret," I'd say, stepping over you.

What did we do all day, with those gloriously empty summer days? Weekends from April to September, holidays, ten-day stretches all summer long for fifteen years, until the rest of us got jobs and you were left alone with Mom and Dad. But while we had them, there were hundreds of those days. No chores, no school, no lessons, no road, no car. Just books and music and the woods behind the house and the faint trail left by the invisible deer. We sat on the beach, dug in our toes, swam in the cool slippery water. As teenagers we spent hours on the long cedar dock, playing our music, our baby-oil-slathered bodies glistening in the sun. Our mother would call from the porch to ask if we had sunscreen on. Yes, we'd lie.

But where were you? Sometimes with us, hardly ever joining us of your own accord. More often you preferred to be by yourself, playing records. Or Mom would coax you out in the rowboat. In the evenings we played cards, board games, read some more. You listened to your music. We went to bed early. It sounds so uneventful, but even when we were too young to really appreciate it, we cherished that time. I think those hundreds of empty days gave us a space for contemplation and rest that would help us later. Maybe if things had been different, we'd have all been artists and writers and musicians. As it turned out, the quiet at least helped balance out the chaos and the violence in our lives, gave us a well to drop down into when there was too much screaming. Like leaping off the dock and landing at the bottom of the lake, resting easy in the silent, waving seaweed.

I'd like to reclaim one of those days. Just one. Twenty-four hours in total, including not-too-hot languorous daytime hours that stretched long and thin like a blissful cat warming herself on tile steps. I'd like the sun-soaked hours full of onshore breeze, swooping barn swallows, and the smell of pine trees and lilacs. Afternoon twilight, squeaking bats, darkness, and the sound of the waves lapping the shore. Our mother's voice before we fell asleep saying, "Listen to the water go splash, splash." I'd give up the nighttime interruptions, the door slamming and the yelling, your laughter and the creak of the bedsprings as you dashed back into your room, Dad erupting in anger, Mom mediating endlessly.

I'd keep this day in a jar on my desk so that I could take it out and remember. Put my hand in and stir it around to feel that way again. Keep it in my pocket and touch it now and again as I walked the streets of my neighborhood in Oregon. Remember the way it felt to be young, unaware, in love with the morning. And waiting for you to wake up.

. . .

TELLING LIES CAME early for me. Almost earlier than memory. This untruth: Louie did it. My mother asks who put the teeth marks in your arm. She's pulled back the flannel sleeve of your nightgown to reveal the curved red circle, clearly the imprint of my three-year-old mouth, but I blame it on the ancient dachshund who sits blinking up at me. I had to make you be quiet. It didn't work, my teeth in your arm only made you cry harder, but then I was the one in trouble. Later, when the other dog bites me in the face, I figure it is payback.

I always felt like I had to make you be quiet. *Why can't you shut up?* There is the rocking and wailing for hours, the screaming and banging. You can't tell us what you want. Maybe it is a small piece of plastic you've treasured for days and dropped somewhere. Maybe your skin hurts, or the noise is bothering you. We'll never know. And we'll never be able to do more than wait it out.

At the lake you scream and scream, and none of us can get away, because there is no road and no neighbors and no way to make you stop. Dad is so angry, again. *Why can't you shut up?* And I'm angry and afraid and helpless. For a few minutes, I hate you. I imagine how satisfying it would be to slug you in the stomach. I imagine the look on your face after my small balled-up fist punches you there. And then I do it. And you're stunned, the wind knocked out of you, and when your breath comes back, you cry even harder. Then I hate myself more than I ever hated you.

Later, much later, you come to visit me in Seattle with Mom. We're at the Coastal Kitchen, and you won't stop laughing, spraying water across the table in my face. I wanted to bring Mom here, and Mom brought you, and now you are ruining everything. I know how much it will hurt you, my heavy shoe slamming into your delicate shin, before I kick you. And I do it anyway. Now your laughter has turned to wailing. And I am sickened by my own nature. It's been almost fifteen years, and I can still see you, open-mouthed and sobbing as you clutch your shin. What kind of a sister am I?

You shoved me, pinched me, spanked me, smacked me on top of the head, pulled my hair, grabbed my neck, kicked me for decades. A couple of years ago you kneed me in the face when I hunched down next to your chair, trying to calm you down. I fell and hit my head on the tile patio.

But all of that was different coming from you. You couldn't control yourself. Sometimes you were trying to be funny. Other times you wanted me and everyone else to get the hell away from you as you grappled with some nameless anxiety; the last thing you needed was someone in your face.

The physical struggle leaves an imprint. It's a violent intimacy that we carry in our history. The pain in my neck, I can feel it now. The red tattoo of my teeth on your arm. Your stomach, my face. Your shin, my heart. I want to heal that history and replace it with a gentler one.

That is the challenge, then, the desire to make whatever future we might have as a family different from the past. Your disorder—autism—brought so much sadness into my life. It took away the sister I could have had and replaced her with you, locked away inside yourself. Sometimes you'd show yourself, waving at me from behind the bars. But mostly it was battle. Autism took away the family we could have had and replaced it with seven struggling individuals alienated from each other by the same enemy. I always thought I just needed to try harder: If I only try harder, I will find Margaret in there somewhere. If I try harder, we will get along and be happy. I'm just not being patient enough, smart enough, diligent enough. I'm borne forward on the false hope that you will get better someday. Somehow there will be a measurable improvement if I just keep trying. Be a better sister. Help your sister. Take care of your sister. You're not trying hard enough.

Just the other day, you sat on my couch here in Oregon listening to June Carter Cash's *Wildwood* CD for the fifth time in a row. You were calm, lightly patting a throw pillow to the beat of the music, head cocked, looking at the ceiling. My dog was asleep with her head on your lap. I looked at you and thought, *This is it. This is you, and here I am. This is what we've got. And it's got to be enough, because it's all there is.*

I'D ALWAYS WANTED to believe that there was some magic to your disability, some deeper meaning in the barrier that separates you from the rest of us, like opaque, wavy glass on the principal's office door. For years I held on to the notion that this obstacle and my constant, fruitless attempts to overcome it somehow made our lives more important, gave our suffering a spiritual dimension. I was waiting for the Disney ending when the Virgin of Lourdes would walk down off the stained-glass window in the church, bless you with the holy waters, and call you healed.

Then one day I realized that I had been completely wrong about all of it. Your autism was nothing special. Nor was the chaos it brought into our family. It was just life. We had it worse than some, better than others. There was nothing to wait for. This was it.

Considering how long I'd clutched that other flag, I surrendered it with surprising ease, tossed it aside like an old newspaper, brushed my hands together, and got on with things. In my case, getting on with things meant claiming my life for myself, the life I'd put on hold for so many years while I was waiting for the grand finale. I'd spent years worrying about what I was supposed to do to save you, never realizing there was nothing I *could* do. I kept a corner of my mind so busy with worry that it felt like I was doing something important, but it was just static. I wasn't actually doing anything for you. Just worrying away the time, my life, yours.

I had to face the fact that whatever became of me would come from me and noplace else. My interests, talents, and inclinations finally claimed my life for their own and began to marshal my days and years with meaning. I've had to sort out my desires and motivations to construct my own compass, replacing what had been there before—an empty sense of obligation—with the everyday reality of my own, ordinary life. I find that if I trust myself and take my time, I tend to move in the right direction, and I don't seem to keep running off three ways at once.

And then here you are. Now that I don't have to spend all that time worrying about you, I have begun to see you more clearly. There is our history—your life, my life, and the interwoven patterns of our shared past with its joy and pain. But mostly there is just you—very alive and in the present. You are a living, breathing woman, who is also trying to make her own way in the world. It has become apparent that there is this opportunity, this new endeavor. After all this time, I have the strange and simple challenge of trying to learn how to be your sister.

WE ARE RIDING together in the car. I'm thirty-five and I'm driving. You are thirty-nine and silent. We are traveling at top speed down the Columbia River Gorge as I drive you back toward your home in eastern Washington. We're listening to classic rock, because that's the only station we can get on this highway cut deep into the basalt canyon dividing Washington from Oregon. We have water on one side, cliffs on the other, and we are racing east.

You're tapping a balled fist softly against your knee. I look at you, my big sister, your short brown hair the exact color of mine. As I've aged, my brown eyes have lightened to match your hazel ones.

We can't offer each other much. I've always wanted to make your life better, but I don't know if that is even possible. I have no idea what you would want for me or if you are even capable of such an estimation. But I do know at least that you wanted to come visit me, that you wanted to stay, and you are happy, now, to let me drive you home. My heart is full of all I can't say to you, because you wouldn't understand, because you would rather ride in silence. Still, I see you there.

"Hi, Margaret," I say.

You look at me. "Hi, Eileen."

We are quiet again. I'm watching the ribbon of the road racing toward us through the windshield.

"Hi, Eileen," you say again.

"Hi, Margs."

I'm listening. I wonder what you are thinking, where your mind goes as you lean your head against the window and watch the white line on the side of the highway as it glides past the car.

"Hi," you say.

I look at you. You point to the radio.

"That's Aerosmith, Eileen."

This makes me laugh.

What would Steven Tyler say? You can't call me on the phone or tell me you love me. You can't even tell me what you did last week, but you can recognize Aerosmith anywhere.

"Yep, that's Aerosmith, Margs," I tell you.

"That's Aerosmith."

"Yes, that's Aerosmith."

"You're listening to Aerosmith, Eileen."

"Yes, Margaret. We're listening to Aerosmith."

We pass this piece of information back and forth between us like a bit of magic. It's a piece of treasure, a soap bubble catching all the colors of the rainbow. And, working together, we keep it up in the air.

I'll think of this moment in years to come when we are suffering through a rough spot brought on by one of your moods. When you don't want to talk to me, or when you want to go home early even though I just drove three hundred miles to see you.

I will think of it during the times when you are quiet and happy, when you reach out to take my hand as we walk up to the house, when you sit next to me in a bar listening to a blues band, when you call good night to me from my guest room.

I will feel it reverberate—our own hard-won and fragile joy, the thrum of the undeniable bond that links us. It's a fragile borderland between hope and change. I cling to that and try to believe that it might bleed over into the rest of my life.

You have made my life indescribably different from what I could ever have imagined. I may have given up expecting much from you, and I know things could fall apart at any moment. But I've come to understand that you are making an effort to let me into your life, just as I am creating a place for you in mine. Sometimes, I can simply absorb the grace of it all—the simple fact that we are sitting next to each other sharing the same moment.

Last fall during your visit, we climbed a steep flight of stairs from downtown to my neighborhood and were both winded when we reached the top. As the ground flattened out you reached over, twined your slender fingers in mine, and asked me if we were going to have dinner. I assured you that we were.

You looked worried, your eyes searching mine. I know you just wanted to know what came next. So do I.

resources

BOOKS ABOUT SIBLINGS AND FAMILIES

Being the Other One: Growing up with a Brother or Sister Who Has Special Needs, Kate Strohm (Shambhala Publications, 2005)

A Difference in the Family: Living with a Disabled Child, Dr. Helen Featherstone (Penguin Books, 1982)

The Normal One: Life with a Difficult or Damaged Sibling, Jeanne Safer (Free Press, 2002)

Siblings of Children with Autism: A Guide for Families, Sandra L. Harris and Beth Glasberg (Woodbine House, 2003)

BOOKS BY SIBLINGS

Boy Alone: A Brother's Memoir, Karl Taro Greenfeld (Harper Collins Publishers, 2009)

The Ride Together: A Brother and Sister's Memoir of Autism in the Family, Paul and Judy Karasik (Washington Square Press, 2002)

Riding the Bus with My Sister: A True Life Journey, Rachel Simon (Plume, 2002)

That Went Well: Adventures in Caring for My Sister, Terrell Harris Dougan (Hyperion, 2009)

Thicker Than Water: Essays by Adult Siblings of People with Disabilities, edited by Don Meyer (Woodbine House, 2009) resources

BOOKS BY ADULTS WITH AUTISM

Emergence: Labeled Autistic, Temple Grandin and Margaret Scariano (Warner Books, 1996)

Nobody Nowhere: The Extraordinary Autobiography of an Autistic, Donna Williams (Perennial, 2002)

Send in the Idiots: Stories from the Other Side of Autism, Kamran Nazeer (Bloomsbury, 2006)

Thinking in Pictures and Other Reports from My Life with Autism, Temple Grandin (Doubleday, 1995)

BOOKS BY PARENTS

Exiting Nirvana: A Daughter's Life with Autism, Clara Claiborne Park (Little, Brown, 2001)

Let Me Hear Your Voice: A Family's Triumph over Autism, Catherine Maurice (Ballantine Books, 1993)

Making Peace with Autism: One Family's Story of Struggle, Discovery, and Unexpected Gifts, Susan Senator (Trumpeter, 2006)

The Siege: A Family's Journey Into the World of an Autistic Child, Clara Claiborne Park (Back Bay Books, 1982)

MOVIES

Autism: The Musical, 2007

The Black Balloon, 2008

The Keys to the House, 2004

Rain Main, 1988

What's Eating Gilbert Grape, 1993

acknowledgments

THIS BOOK COULD not have been written without the help and encouragement of the many special people I am lucky enough to have in my life. I would like to express my deepest gratitude to: Anne Bartlett Blair, my generous and kind first reader; Larry Garvin, for being the family filter and for giving unexpected and insightful comments about the writing itself; Beth Award, who has listened to my stories for years and whose friendship I cannot do without; Steve Zaro, faithful friend and sage, who always steers me right; the Sol Sisters, who inspire me to be the person they think I am; my family, Lawrence Garvin, Patricia Garvin, Mike Garvin, Larry Garvin, and Ann Modarelli, for their love and support; my grandmother, Patricia Travis, for feeding me books and telling me I would be a writer; Terrell Harris Dougan, fellow sibling and bridge to the book world; Laura Yorke and Matthew Lore, for believing in this story; Brendan Ramey, for inexhaustible love and support; and Margaret Garvin, who taught me how to read the world.

about the author

EILEEN GARVIN WAS born and raised in the Pacific Northwest. The youngest of five children, she has always been close with her sister Margaret, who is three years her senior and was diagnosed with autism the month Eileen was born. She writes for newspapers, magazines, and Web sites from Hood River, Oregon, where she lives with her husband, Brendan. This is her first book.